Applied Ethics Primer

APPLIED ETHICS PRIMER

LETITIA MEYNELL
AND CLARISSE PARON

BROADVIEW PRESS

BROADVIEW PRESS – www.broadviewpress.com
Peterborough, Ontario, Canada

Founded in 1985, Broadview Press remains a wholly independent publishing house. Broadview's focus is on academic publishing; our titles are accessible to university and college students as well as scholars and general readers. With over 800 titles in print, Broadview has become a leading international publisher in the humanities, with world-wide distribution. Broadview is committed to environmentally responsible publishing and fair business practices.

© 2023 Letitia Meynell and Clarisse Paron

Library and Archives Canada Cataloguing in Publication

Title: Applied ethics primer / Letitia Meynell and Clarisse Paron.
Names: Meynell, Letitia, author. | Paron, Clarisse, author.
Description: Includes bibliographical references.
Identifiers: Canadiana (print) 20230219683 | Canadiana (ebook) 20230219713 | ISBN 9781554816149 (softcover) | ISBN 9781770488991 (PDF) | ISBN 9781460408315 (EPUB)
Subjects: LCSH: Applied ethics.
Classification: LCC BJ1031 .M49 2023 | DDC 170—dc23

Broadview Press handles its own distribution in North America:
PO Box 1243, Peterborough, Ontario K9J 7H5, Canada
555 Riverwalk Parkway, Tonawanda, NY 14150, USA
Tel: (705) 743-8990; Fax: (705) 743-8353
email: customerservice@broadviewpress.com

For all territories outside of North America, distribution is handled by Eurospan Group.

Canada

Broadview Press acknowledges the financial support of the Government of Canada for our publishing activities.

Edited by Robert M. Martin
Book design by Michel Vrana

PRINTED IN CANADA

Contents

Acknowledgements

We gratefully acknowledge support from Dalhousie University Libraries and Centre for Learning and Teaching through the Open Educational Resources (OER) Grant and Geoff Brown's invaluable guidance in the production of the online version of this resource. The primer itself has been greatly improved by feedback from countless colleagues, including Jackie Alvarez, Melany Banks, Oliver Boettcher, Andrew Fenton, Landon Gaetz, Leaf Kretz, Lynette Reid, Meredith Schwartz, Andrea Sullivan-Clarke, Kira Tomsons, Sandra Tomsons, Charissa Varma, as well as Dalhousie students in Philosophy 1050/2680 Ethics in Science and audiences at the Canadian Philosophical Association, the Canadian Society for the Study of Practical Ethics, and the Dalhousie Philosophy Colloquium. We especially thank Bob Martin, Tara Lowes, and Joe Davies for their close and thoughtful reading as well as Stephen Latta for his enthusiasm for the project and patience with us.

Finally, we also acknowledge that this work was produced in an institution that rests on unceded Mi'kmaq territory. We recognize the legal status of the Treaties of Peace and Friendship, first signed by the Mi'kmaq, Wəlastəkwiyik, Peskotomuhkati, and the British Crown in 1726, even as we struggle to understand what this means for us all.

Online Content

The notes and further readings sections of this book include links to many online resources. For convenience these links are provided separately at the following website:

sites.broadviewpress.com/ethicsprimer

Part I

INTRODUCTION

Over the years, many branches of **applied ethics** have emerged. If you look at a university calendar you may find courses on computer ethics, environmental ethics, business ethics, and professional ethics, to name but a few. There are even subdisciplines within some of these branches. For instance, within bioethics one can now find research ethics, gen-ethics, and health care ethics, and the list continues. If you are beginning to suspect that there is no type of activity that doesn't admit some sort of ethical analysis, then you're right. This is because ethics is a discipline that seeks to answer what is at once a simple, yet extremely difficult, question: What should I (or we) do? One might ask instead, "How should we live?" or, "What is a good life?" However, each of these questions is connected to the others and they all can be thought of as asking much the same kind of thing.

It is tempting to rephrase the question "What should I do?" as "What *can* I do?" "What do I *want* to do?" or "What do *other people want* me to do?" If you do this, you are confusing an *ought* with an *is*.[1] You are taking a **normative** question—in other words, a question that concerns what *ought* to be the case or what *ought* to be done—and trying to replace it with a **descriptive** question about some fact of the matter. In the case of the rephrased questions above, what is within my capacity, what I desire, or what other people desire, respectively.

Changing the normative question from what I or we or you (or someone else) *should* do to a descriptive question is, in effect, an effort to leave the ethical analysis up to someone else. The idea that this is a way of avoiding ethics is, however, an illusion. Most decision-making has a moral dimension. Part of being a mature, rational individual in a society is being accountable for one's decisions and actions. Even if we don't make the effort to consider whether our actions are right or wrong, others will.

This primer is a resource for helping you notice and attend to ethical issues and think your way through them. The intent is to give you tools to help you figure out what you (or others) *should* do so that you can weigh these moral considerations against what you can do, what you want to do, and what others want you to do. Sometimes you will be fortunate enough to discover that the answers to these questions line up and you are not faced with a problem. All too frequently, however, you will find that if you really think about it, what you want to do or what others want you to do fail to accord with what you *should* do. What you *can* do provides the limit of the actions that are open to you. However, carefully considering ethical challenges can often help us revise our own sense of what is possible and recognize that more may be within our power than we might have initially thought.

This primer will not tell you what to do. That's up to you. Instead, it offers a variety of ways of thinking about ethics for you to apply yourself. Again, rational, adult humans are, and should be, held accountable for their actions. So, being able to articulate ethically sound reasons for your actions is important for being able to defend yourself to others who might disagree with your choices and behaviour.

Of course, context matters. This is one of the reasons why applied ethics subdisciplines abound. Nonetheless, there are commonalities among these areas as they all engage and take guidance from **normative ethical theory**. Normative ethics is the systematic study, development, and rational defence of basic values, moral concepts, and ethical theories. Ethicists offer theories that explain why some actions are right and others wrong and why some states of affairs, institutions or, indeed, people are good and others bad.

For well over 2,000 years, philosophers from around the globe have been writing down what they take to be the right way to live and giving arguments for why we should act in one way or another. Of course, the practice of ethics is considerably older than the written record and has been an essential part of all human cultures for thousands of years. What we address here simply skims the surface of a few of these theories from a handful of cultures. There is a predominance of theories from the European tradition, which reflects the discourses that have shaped most applied ethics written in English. This should not be taken to imply that the basic ideas in these theories are uniquely European nor that they are in some sense superior to their non-European counterparts.

We are currently in an era of post-colonial correction, and we can expect that many non-European theories will increasingly inform applied ethics. Moreover, the basic approaches discussed below can be found throughout ethical theories globally. So, along with some key figures and theories from European ethics, we will discuss ideas from various so-called "non-Western" traditions.

So, what are the kinds of tools that moral philosophers can offer? First are generic philosophical tools of careful criticism, including the analysis of important concepts, and argumentation. These are skills that are crucial to any philosophical work, which students would acquire and practice in any philosophy course. Second, there are the theories that moral philosophers have developed. Although there are many different theories, we will organize them into four basic approaches that focus on different things: consequences; action; character; and relationships. Many ethical theories actually touch on all of these aspects but emphasize one of them as a central focus or starting point. Some moral frameworks and concepts don't neatly fit into any one of these four approaches, and we will discuss two of these—rights theory and *ahimsa*—after the rest.

Rather than offering a set of arguments about why one theory is superior to another, we will treat our four approaches as different lenses through which we can assess the various cases and situations that attract our attention.[2] Just as looking at a landscape through lenses that are tinted different colours makes different features stand out, so thinking about ethical challenges through each of the basic approaches draws attention to certain moral features of these situations. In this way, employing these lenses can improve our moral perception, helping us notice and analyze ethical issues and envision more effective ways of addressing them.

Now, one might think that one of these theories is in fact the *correct* account of morality. Indeed, many normative ethicists take this view and spend their careers defending one or other moral theory. Even so, it is still important to understand other theories to be able to sympathetically consider and assess other people's approaches to moral problems. Before we get to the ethical lenses in Part II, we will reflect on the character of moral judgement and present some tools for argumentation and debate.

1
Moral Response and Reflection

1.1 Moral Response

Often when we make moral judgements, we find they are tied up with our emotional reactions. For instance, we typically feel happy when good things happen to good people and angry when we witness things that are unjust. We may also feel personal satisfaction at having done the right thing and pride in having it recognized. Similarly, we often feel guilt for acting badly and shame when others call us out for it. These familiar experiences are moral judgements just as much as emotional reactions.

Although emotions can be important and instructive by alerting us to moral issues, they are sometimes not well justified on reflection. Indeed, in some instances, once we reflect on our emotions, we may find that they are ethically quite misleading. Even positive emotions, like love, may lead us to misjudge a situation, prompting us to defend friends or family members who have, in fact, behaved badly. Negative emotions can be equally misleading. Most of us have had the experience of being in a fit of anger and doing something (or at least thinking of doing something) that we later recognize was morally wrong. The Roman historian Tacitus believed that many people have a tendency to hate those whom they have injured.[1] Our emotional reactions to our own bad behaviour might distort our perception of our victims in ways that would make us prone to harm them yet further. This should trouble anyone who is inclined to let their emotions govern their actions. Indeed, philosophical traditions that foreground moral emotions tend to emphasize the importance of cultivating virtuous or appropriate emotional responses (as we will see in Chapter 5).

If our emotions can be fallible guides to moral action, what else might we consider? We might think about how others will judge our actions or how they would act were they in our place. Again, this can be instructive in terms of alerting us to moral considerations (as we shall see in section 5.3 and section 6.1). Nonetheless, this is typically insufficient for coming to a justified moral judgement. There are good reasons for this. There are many biases in our society and many people who behave badly. If we simply judge as others judge and follow what others do or what they expect us to do, we may end up making some terrible judgements and engaging in some heinous behaviour.

It can be deeply disturbing to discover that those who hold a respected place in our community or the people we love have immoral attitudes or have engaged in morally repugnant behaviour. Nonetheless, if we truly care about doing the right thing, we must be open to making such discoveries. We may even discover that attitudes or conventions that are widely accepted in our society are nonetheless morally pernicious.

Of course, many social conventions are perfectly morally acceptable. Some may even be morally required. After all, conventional norms and practices offer a set of rules for behaviour that help the members of society understand one another and fruitfully interact with each other. However, in order to be able to distinguish conventions that are useful and good from those that are bigoted and bad we need to go beyond the conventions themselves. This is where normative ethics, philosophical analysis, and argument come in.

Stop and Think

Take a moment to consider a norm or a practice that was (or perhaps is) thought to be ethically acceptable in some culture or society (perhaps even your own) that you believe is morally wrong.

Now try to articulate the reasons why it's wrong.

You have just started doing moral philosophy!

1.2   Reflection

Now, one might wonder how we can discover that we ourselves or members of our community have been following customs that are morally wrong, if we are located in societies and communities that follow these customs. This is where moral theory, conceptual analysis, and argumentation come in. We can use these to assess the norms, conventions, and practices of our own communities. Even so, it is difficult to understand how things might be different from within our own culture. This is where outside perspectives are particularly valuable.

As a number of philosophers who study the **theory of knowledge** have argued, the critical eye of people with very different beliefs, norms, and values from our own can be extremely useful for assessing the claims we endorse and the things we do. The idea is that if a claim or practice can withstand criticism from a wide variety of different perspectives with very different assumptions then it must be pretty good, or at least it is likely to be morally acceptable. It is rather like using various experiments to test the same hypothesis. If your hypothesis is confirmed using a wide array of very different experimental designs, then your scientific investigations have given you good reason for thinking it is likely right.

Notice, that this process does not give us grounds for dogmatically claiming the matter is permanently decided in either science or ethics. Moreover, our assessments must be done in good faith. If we value scientific knowledge, we should welcome having multiple rigorous tests of our favoured theories. In the same way, if we want to do the right thing, we should be open to criticism from a wide variety of different people whose views are very different from our own. Of course, others may or may not be right in their criticisms. Either way, being able to understand and assess them will give us insight into the relevant ethical issues and better justification for our own ethical decisions.

Unfortunately, we often don't have access to a variety of people from many different backgrounds to give us feedback on our ideas and activities. Even if we do, these folks may have better things to do than help us with our moral dilemmas. Fortunately, we do have access to published work by thinkers from around the globe and we can draw on this and our own imaginations to guess what those who disagree with us might say. This kind of **dialogic reasoning** is characteristic of philosophical work (as we will see in Chapter 2). If you want to do the right thing then sincerely considering arguments both for and against the various possible actions that are open to you is one of the best ways of ensuring that you do.

Stop and Think

Can you remember a moment of your life in which someone
with a completely different background or perspective said or
did something that prompted you to reconsider one of your own
cherished ethical or political commitments?

What was the difference that made the difference?

If you have never had such an experience, why do you think that
might be?

Now, it might reasonably be asked whether such a process of rational reflection, judgement, and action will always provide the right answer. Philosophers have disagreed on this point. However, the very fact of their disagreement suggests that, for practical purposes, all philosophers are going to have to admit that seemingly rational people do *in fact* disagree about moral issues and sometimes these disagreements are intractable.

1.3   Disagreement

It is worth articulating the different ways in which philosophers disagree, as this will help us better analyze and assess competing theories. Sometimes philosophers disagree about the facts. For instance, two philosophers might share the same basic normative views but disagree about relevant features of the world. Suppose two philosophers agree that what matters morally is to make people as happy as possible. However, one believes that, psychologically speaking, what actually makes people happy is ensuring their safety, while the other believes that happiness depends on maximizing people's freedom. Both agree that happiness is a particular emotional state, but they disagree about the facts regarding what causes it. Notice that if they both really care about doing the right thing, they are probably going to want to look at some empirical work here. For example, they might examine research in social psychology to see what really does make people happy.

Another possibility is that the philosophers disagree about what happiness *means* or, alternatively, what *type* of happiness is morally relevant. One philosopher might think that *true happiness* is an emotional state that is experienced moment to moment while the other might think that *true happiness* depends on achievement and overcoming various struggles and obstacles over a lifetime. These philosophers are effectively disagreeing about what a certain concept means. Scientific investigations are unlikely to be helpful. In order for science to discover what causes happiness, first it must be determined what we're talking about when we refer to *happiness*. This brings us back into the realm of philosophy.

Notice that this question about what a moral concept means is intimately related to *who counts*. Here, again, our philosophers might disagree. After all, many nonhuman animals appear to experience emotional states like happiness, in which case the first philosopher should, presumably, include these animals in their moral decision-making. The second philosopher might not agree. They might argue that other animals can't formulate the kinds of life projects that are required for happiness, and claim that only humans (or perhaps most humans and a handful of other species) count.[2] While the sciences might be invaluable for identifying which animals (and humans) have the capacity to be happy, they can only do this work after philosophers have defined it.

Finally, we might simply accept different moral theories and values or rank them differently in importance. One philosopher might think that maximizing happiness is the single most important moral goal while another thinks it is irrelevant because freedom is the only thing that matters morally, whether it makes people happy or not. Here again, there is philosophical work to be done.

Summary of the Types of Moral Disagreement

Disagreement about the facts

Disagreement about what a key philosophical term means

Disagreement about who counts

Disagreement about which moral theories or values are right or relevant

Notice that *if we agree about the facts, the meaning of moral concepts, who counts, and the applicable moral theory or values, we should agree about the right course of action.* If we are reasoning carefully and disagree about the right course of action it is almost certainly because we disagree about the relevant facts, the meaning of moral concepts, who counts, or the relevant moral theories or values (or their relative importance).

Importantly, whatever we decide to do, we are morally responsible for that decision and its outcome—good or bad. *We should expect to be held accountable for our actions.* Happily, if we have carefully considered our options, listened to and learned from those who disagree, and looked at the situation through each ethical lens and from all relevant perspectives, we can expect to have a robust and convincing justification for our actions.

In applied contexts, there is the possibility that even if we *disagree* about the facts, the interpretation of moral concepts, who counts, and the correct normative theories, we may nonetheless *agree* about what the right action is in a given situation. This gives us another reason for not just choosing one lens or theory over the others but instead taking a more pluralist approach. If we can show that the same action is required by a broad set of very different moral views, then this becomes very powerful evidence that the action is morally required. So, even if you are inclined to think that one of the approaches discussed below is right to the exclusion of the others, you may be able to provide far more compelling arguments if you notice when they agree.

Chapter 1 Quiz

1. There are several ways that philosophers might have disagreements that are discussed in the *Applied Ethics Primer*. Which of the following is *not* one of them.
    a. This question is misleading, philosophers never disagree.
    b. We can disagree about the facts.
    c. We can disagree about which moral theory is correct.
    d. We can disagree about the interpretation of a theory or concept.

2. True or False: Normative ethical theory is the systematic study, development, and rational defence of basic values, moral concepts, and ethical theories.

3. True or False: A *descriptive question* addresses what ought to be the case or what ought to be done.

2
Reason and Argument

2.1 Reason

The subject of disagreement is intimately related to argument. If we are reasonable, we will, presumably, have reasons for our decisions and actions. If we want to convince others that these decisions and actions are right, then we will want to put these reasons into a logical order so that they form a strong argument. Logic is a subdiscipline of philosophy that is as old as ethics. Like ethics, logic has a global history woven into parallel histories of rhetoric and theories about language. Although formal logic has dominated discussions of logic in the European tradition for the last two centuries, it tends to have a limited application in applied ethics discussions. So, we will take a rather broader approach that includes, but is not restricted to, some of the inference patterns of formal logic.

At this point, we're inclined to direct you to a classic skit by the British comedy troupe, Monty Python. In their "Argument Sketch,"[1] they discuss and exemplify both what philosophical argument is and what it isn't. Part of what they play with is the fact that we use the word "argument" in a number of different ways. We can see three different senses of the term in the skit, only two of which are philosophical. The first sense is when people who disagree about something (or think they disagree) yell at each other. This is not the philosophical sense of argument. It is correlated with it, however, as sometimes people who are engaged in such yelling matches at least started out with each taking up a contrary position and trying to convince the other.

This second sense of argument is basically a synonym for debate. Two or more parties—interlocutors—take up contrary positions on a point and try to convince the other(s). This is "an intellectual process," as one of the characters points out, and a practice that is crucial to philosophy. It is not mere contradiction because *reasons* are given in an effort to change the other's mind.

Even when there is no other person around, philosophers will often think of and defend their own positions with a type of internal debate. They themselves take up a contrary position to their own view, make as good a case as possible for it, only to defeat it later. This is one of the reasons that you need to pay careful attention when reading philosophy. It is all too easy to mistake a passage where an author is explaining an objection to their position as an account of their own view (in philosophy, we call this process **dialogic reasoning**). If you are not used to reading philosophy this can seem bizarre. Why would someone argue against their own view just to show that the argument they have given does not work? The idea is, if you can correctly articulate your opponent's reasons for disagreeing with you and then show that either there is a flaw in this reasoning or that it is insufficient to dislodge your claim, then you effectively undermine their position and support your own. The point of debate is to convince other people of your own view or discover errors in your thinking and revise it. So, considering objections—thinking about why others might disagree with you and what you can say in response—is crucial for philosophical argumentation.

This brings us to our third sense of argument. These are the parts of the argument in the debate sense. Here, Monty Python offers a definition that you might find in any introductory logic book: "An argument is a connected series of statements to establish a definite proposition." Often philosophers will call the connected series of statements "**premises**," though this is really just a fancy word for reasons. The "definite proposition," or "**conclusion**," is established by the premises. (This use of the term "conclusion" can sometimes be a bit confusing as the same word is also used to refer to the final section of an essay.) Philosophers often use this language of premises and conclusion, but it is important not to let these technical terms intimidate you. A conclusion is just a controversial statement that you are trying to convince others to believe, and the premises are the reasons that you give for holding it. Sometimes it can be tricky to determine what the conclusion is, but often authors will use verbal signs, predicating their conclusion with "thus," "therefore," "hence," or a phrase like "it follows that." (You can find a list of these kinds of verbal signs in Appendix A, Tips for Reading Actively.)

It is important to note that a philosopher will often have multiple conclusions and arguments in their paper, though typically these all serve to defend one central conclusion.

Summary of the Three Senses of "Argument"

Yelling match—mere contradiction

Debate—two or more parties trying to convince each other of opposing positions

Philosophical argument—a connected series of premises given to establish a conclusion

Another useful point we can find in Monty Python's "Argument Sketch" is the distinction between an argument and a *good* argument. Of course, in the sketch, when one of the characters says, "I came here for a good argument," he means something like he was expecting a debate that was interesting and fun. Because we are more concerned with the third type of argument, we are going to think about good arguments as ones that are successful. That is, a good argument is one that would convince any rational person of the truth (or reasonableness) of the conclusion. The premises of a *good* argument really do establish the conclusion (or at least show it to be more reasonable than alternatives).

2.2   How to Evaluate Philosophical Arguments

Now, it is all very well to say this, but we still need more guidance as to how to assess arguments. Again, there is a huge and diverse global literature on this very topic. Nonetheless, most of it can be summarized (albeit superficially) in a neat heuristic offered by Canadian philosopher, Trudy Govier. She suggests that we evaluate arguments by posing three different questions about the premises and their relation to the conclusion, which she calls the *ARG conditions*: **A**, are the premises true or at least *acceptable*? **R**, are the premises *relevant* to the conclusion? **G**, do the premises provide *good grounds* for accepting the conclusion?[2] (See Appendix B: Critical Thinking Worksheet for an interactive resource to help you assess whether an argument adequately meets the ARG conditions. It can also be used to help you develop your own philosophical arguments.)

The first condition—**A**, the truth or acceptability of the premises—is pretty easy to understand. If the reasons that someone gives for believing a particular conclusion are *false* (or otherwise unacceptable), then you don't have any reason for accepting that conclusion. Ideally, we would be certain that each premise is true, but certain truth is a difficult standard to maintain. After all, even very well verified and widely accepted claims in the sciences—for instance, that cigarette smoking causes cancer—might just be false. This is not a flaw of science; it is a side effect of the empirical and statistical methods that are characteristic of scientific research. It is *possible*, albeit extraordinarily unlikely, that every study of the issue had some unrecognized fatal flaw and that the well-evidenced correlation between cigarette smoking and cancer is the result of some other factor or factors that are correlated with cigarette smoking, and that actually cause cancer. Nonetheless, it is *reasonable* to accept the claim that cigarette smoking causes cancer even if we don't have absolute certainty. Indeed, if we are not willing to accept claims like this, we will find it difficult to make any ethical decisions at all (or, indeed, any other kind of decision).

At the same time, we do want to avoid uncritically accepting everything that someone says to defend their position. Thus, it is important to reflect on why each premise is acceptable and to sincerely question whether, in fact, more information is needed before a rational evaluation of a given premise can be made.

The second condition—**R**, the relevance of the premises—is a bit trickier. It may seem obvious that for a premise to establish a conclusion it must be relevant, but, in fact, people quite often use irrelevant facts to try to convince others to think or do something. There are many different ways of distracting people from carefully thinking through the matter at hand and irrelevant premises tend to do this. One of our favourite examples is a **false equivalency** that is used in an antacid commercial from the 1990s.[3] In this commercial, a man first dips a rose into a glass of hydrochloric acid, visibly damaging the rose. He then dips a second rose into the same acid, but only after first coating it in the antacid product being advertised. The second rose emerges seemingly unharmed.

We can reconstruct the argument offered by the commercial as something like this:

Premise 1. If we dip a rose in acid the acid will eat away the rose.

Premise 2. But if we coat the rose in this particular brand of antacid before dipping it in acid the acid will not eat away the rose.

Conclusion. Therefore, if you have acid indigestion you should "coat" your stomach with this particular brand of antacid.

Of course, a rose is nothing like the human stomach. On the face of it, the fact that the rose is protected by a particular brand of antacid is just not relevant to whether it will help with acid indigestion. Minimally, we need some additional reason to think that it *is* acceptable to "think of this rose as your stomach," as the commercial suggests. That means that for this argument to work you would need to add some reason (or reasons) for thinking that roses and human stomachs are relevantly similar. As it stands, the premises aren't relevant to the conclusion.

The third condition—**G**, whether the premises provide good grounds for accepting the conclusion—is the most general as it includes the other two conditions. After all, premises that aren't true (or at least reasonable) and premises that aren't relevant cannot provide good grounds for accepting a conclusion. Indeed, you may think that if all the premises are true (or at least acceptable) and relevant then they *must* provide good grounds for accepting the conclusion. This, however, is not the case.

Consider a friend who urges you to try taking a herbal remedy the next time you get a cold. The reason they give is that they have started taking it when they get a cold and it works for them. It may well be true that it works for them and it's certainly relevant to the broader question of whether one should try the remedy oneself, but is it good enough grounds for doing so?

You might ask your friend how they came across this remedy. In effect, what you would be doing here is seeing if there are better reasons for taking the remedy. Suppose they say some dude at the farmer's market was selling it and swore by it as the best cold remedy he had ever tried. Do you have better grounds for thinking it will work? On one hand, you now know that there are at least two people who say it works, but on the other hand, you know that one of them has a vested interest as he is selling it. Suppose, instead, that your friend cites a meta-analysis of 20 randomized control trials showing the efficacy of the remedy for various cold viruses and across various population groups. Now, clearly, that's much better grounds for thinking that the remedy will work for you than simply the testimony of either your friend or the dude at the farmer's market.

When it comes to some applied ethics contexts, we will find that what constitutes good enough grounds depends on the seriousness of a situation and the risks involved should we make a bad choice. With the question of whether you should take the herbal remedy at your friend's urging, the stakes are pretty low. After all, they're still alive, so you can infer that it's likely not poisonous. The worst thing that is likely to happen is that it just won't make any difference to your cold symptoms, and you'll be out a few dollars. But suppose instead that you are a health officer in charge of coordinating a response to a global pandemic in your local area and the president of the United States claims that a particular drug (in which they have a financial interest) has worked for them and can significantly reduce the mortality of those infected with the illness. Does this constitute good grounds for spending a considerable portion of your region's budget on this remedy? Here the stakes are higher. The illness is considerably more dangerous; the decision affects many more people than just you; you are in a position of public trust; it's your job to make these kinds of decisions well; millions of dollars will be diverted from other priorities and treatments for the pandemic should you buy the drug; and so on. When the stakes are high it is reasonable to expect people to have *very* good grounds for their conclusions and their decisions.

2.3   How to Engage in Productive Debates

In ethics (and other areas of philosophy), debate has an important role in facilitating the exchange of ideas and providing opportunities for us to learn from each other. However, it is easy to get caught up in the "battle" of argumentation. After all, the first two meanings of the word "argument," discussed above, suggest an antagonistic approach where two (or more) interlocutors take opposing sides on an issue and fight it out. It is especially easy to fall into an adversarial attitude in ethics where we may have strong feelings about right and wrong or have commitments to particular values and important issues may be at stake. In such contexts, it is tempting to try to defend one's own views at all costs. Debate can become emotionally charged, inhibiting our ability to think rationally or listen to the perspectives of others. A focus on winning can distract us from attending to what makes an argument a *good* one—having premises that are acceptable (i.e., true or, at least, reasonable), relevant, and provide good grounds for accepting our conclusion.

There are, however, a couple of things that we can do to make our debates more productive. First, when criticizing someone else's position, we should try to find all the points of agreement. This process will help to narrow down exactly where the disagreement lies and focus the discussion there. Many debates make little progress because people talk past each other; conflicts cannot be resolved because the interlocutors are not arguing about the same thing! (Debates about abortion frequently exemplify this problem as one side focuses on the rights of the pregnant person while the other focuses on the moral status of the fetus.[4])

Second, instead of trying to win, we can engage in **argument repair**.[5] This is where you help your interlocutor make the best case possible for *their* position. Argument repair can be achieved by making assumptions explicit, clarifying ambiguous terms, adding missing premises, or offering subarguments in defence of dubious premises. It is important not to misrepresent the argument when we are trying to repair it, which is easy to do if we disagree.[6] Moreover, for argument repair to be successful, our interlocutor must be open to revising their position and we should allow them an opportunity to do so. Amendments are only justifiable if they make the argument stronger. Added premises must be relevant (it's remarkably easy to get carried away and add irrelevant premises) and provide good grounds for accepting the conclusion and changes should be acceptable to all parties in the debate.

In our everyday conversations, we typically don't state all of the premises needed to give a complete defence of our arguments because we share common background knowledge and assumptions with our interlocutors. However, in more fraught contexts (such as in ethical disputes), there are often unstated premises that aren't shared by all parties or the argument hinges on an important term that each defines in a subtly different way. (We touched on this in the discussion of disagreement in section 1.3.) In these cases, engaging in argument repair can make the debate more productive for everyone by redirecting interlocutors away from an adversarial process to a more collaborative one that is aimed at mutual understanding and a resolution to the dispute that everyone can accept.

Engaging in respectful, good faith dialogue can alert us to features of the moral landscape we may have overlooked or show us how our own reasoning is lacking. We can then use these insights to revise our own views and make the arguments defending them stronger.

2.4 Public Reason

Because applied ethics often addresses issues that affect large groups of people, this constrains what kinds of reasons and ethical theories are appropriate. We need to stand on ethical common ground if our arguments and judgements are to be seen as reasonable or right by others. There are certain theories that, although important in the history of ethics, will not prove fruitful in applied ethics contexts in a pluralist or secular society. These are ethical claims and theories that are based on a commitment to a particular religion. Obviously, some people have deeply held religious convictions and find the laws or principles of their religion a crucial guide for their moral lives. Nonetheless, although such commitments may provide compelling reasons for a practitioner of a given religion, they provide no reason at all for a non-practitioner or someone who is equally strongly committed to an entirely different faith tradition or practice. This is a crucial point because it means that a religious practitioner cannot *justify* their moral claims or decisions to a non-practitioner, so long as they rest only on their religious commitments. Thus, although it may be acceptable to make ethical decisions concerning your own life on the basis of your religious convictions, it is unreasonable to expect others to accept the imposition of ethical prescriptions on them that are based on your (or anyone else's) religion.

A religious practitioner might object that they believe that their religion *does* in fact offer the best guidance for right action, which is why other people should follow their ethical prescriptions. Of course, this is possible. After all, there are many different religious traditions and considerable diversity within each of them and at least some, if not most, of them will have important insights into moral life. The problem is that there is no obvious way to determine *which* religion is the right one and thus which specific ethical rules one should follow.

Mozi, a Chinese philosopher who lived over 2,000 years ago (ca. 480–392? BCE),[7] made a similar point. He argued that it is important that people not simply adopt conventional views and practices—the kinds of practices that people often unthinkingly follow because they were taught them as children—as these practices might not be morally right. Moreover, because people come from different cultures with different practices, simply following these conventions, particularly in contexts of ethical conflict, inevitably leads to social discord and, in some cases, war. Mozi recognized that accepting a kind of **cultural relativism** where right and wrong are simply determined by cultural convention isn't a viable option when people from many different cultures have to live together. Instead, Mozi argued for objective moral standards that everyone should follow.[8]

While Mozi was not an advocate for the kind of general freedom that characterizes contemporary democratic societies, his insights about needing shared ethical standards are still pertinent. This is why applied ethics typically deals with **public reason**. The idea of public reason is that ethical rules and judgements must be acceptable, or at least justifiable, to everyone who is expected to live by them. This means that reasons given in applied ethics contexts should rest on ideas and theories that are not parochial. As we will see when we look at the ethical lenses below, values like rationality, happiness, and freedom have the sort of broad appeal that is characteristic of public reason.

Though not strictly necessary, there is a certain sense of fairness implicit in the idea of public reason. All things being equal, we are all expected to follow the same rules. If there is to be differential treatment, there must be a good reason for it. Indeed, this is really a point about rationality as well as fairness. Like should be treated alike. In ethical contexts, this ideal is called **formal justice**. It is a part of a broader rational norm of consistency.

To summarize, ethics requires us to do more than simply follow our knee-jerk reactions, our emotional responses, or conventional norms when deciding what to do. It is not that they are irrelevant. They can alert us to moral issues and important aspects of a tricky moral dilemma. However, they can also mislead. Moral reasoning requires not only an assessment of the moral issues with a sensitivity to competing analyses but that we have good reasons for what we ultimately decide. We need to commit to shared standards of rational argumentation and constructive debate if we are to defend our judgements and hold each other accountable for our actions. The ethical lenses discussed below help to provide the normative content of these reasons.

Chapter 2 Quiz

1. True or False: Formal justice requires that like should be treated alike.

2. True or False: Every argument that has true and relevant premises will offer good grounds for accepting the conclusion.

3. True or False: The idea of public reason is that the ethical rules in our common life must be acceptable or at least justifiable to everyone who is expected to live by them.

4. True or False: The ARG conditions stand for Acceptable, Rigorous, and Good grounds.

Additional links for Part I are available at:

sites.broadviewpress.com/ethicsprimer/part-1

Part II

ETHICAL LENSES

As mentioned above, there are many different moral theories. As you confront particular moral problems or study applied ethics subdisciplines you will find that digging deeper into these theories is a crucial part of developing your applied ethics toolkit. Nonetheless, at the introductory level we can identify four fundamentally different approaches to moral reasoning that cover the essential ideas of many of these theories:

1. Focus on consequences;
2. Focus on action (and duties);
3. Focus on character (and virtues);
4. Focus on relations.

These are ethical orientations that are woven throughout various global ethical theories and traditions. As noted above, we are going to think of them as lenses that can be brought to the ethical question, what should I (or we) do? A focus on consequences prompts one to evaluate the outcomes of our possible actions, directing us to consider who will be affected in positive or negative ways. A focus on action (and duty) prompts one to think about the actions themselves, what motivates them, and what makes a particular action right or wrong, optional or required. A focus on character (and virtues) presents us with the challenge of figuring out what kind of person we want to be, what constitutes a good life, and the virtues and activities that are characteristic of good people. A focus on relations affirms the importance of relationships of various different kinds and looks at how they inform and constrain what one can and should do. In the next four chapters, we will look at each of these approaches in more detail.

Even as the four lenses offer a comprehensive set of approaches to thinking through ethical problems and issues, some moral concepts defy neat inclusion under one or another lens. We will discuss two important and influential examples—*ahimsa* and rights—in Part III (Chapter 8 and Chapter 9, respectively). As you read about the different lenses (and, indeed, the concepts of *ahimsa* and rights) you will notice that some of the theories offer different views about who or what should be considered when we make ethical decisions. This is captured by the idea of **moral status** (also sometimes called *moral standing* or *moral considerability*). Some theorists treat moral status as a matter of degree, maintaining that some beings have full moral status and their interests should count more in our ethical decision-making, while others still count but to a lesser degree. Other theorists treat moral status as an all-or-nothing kind of issue. What grounds moral status (as we have already seen in section 1.3) is contentious and we will return to it below as we survey the lenses and develop a sense of the ways in which questions about moral status arise.

3

Focus on Consequences

Our first lens focuses on consequences, capturing a set of theories that are classed as types of consequentialism. As we shall see, consequentialists can have very different views of what counts as good or bad consequences. Also, they may think about consequences in quite different ways, with some focusing on individuals and others more interested in groups. Consequentialists also differ in how they factor moral status into decision-making; that is, figuring out who counts. Some consider humans alone while others extend their ethical gaze to include nonhuman animals.

3.1 Mohism

Written consequentialist theories go back to the work of Mozi (mentioned above in section 2.4) and those who followed his work, the Mohists. This philosophical approach saw its zenith during the Warring States era in China (479–221 BCE), a time of political chaos that brought considerable misery and hardship to ordinary people.[1] The right thing to do, according to **Mohism**, is simply to try to alleviate harms done to people and promote what is beneficial to them. Mozi wrote:

> Now at the present time, what brings the greatest harm to
> the world? Great states attacking small ones, great families

overthrowing small ones, the strong oppressing the weak, the many harrying the few, the cunning deceiving the stupid, the eminent lording it over the humble—these are harmful to the world.[2]

Mozi thought that the underlying cause of this misery is that people are partial, meaning that they don't love everyone equally but instead put the interests of particular people—typically, themselves and their loved ones—before everyone else. In a competing approach to ethics in China at the time, love of one's family, especially one's parents (sometimes called **filial piety**) played a central role. Mozi argued that if one really wants to benefit and protect the interests of one's parents, the best way to achieve this is to make sure that everyone else wants it too. The question is how to secure this goal. He explains, "Obviously, I must make it a point to love and benefit other [people's] parents, so that they in return will love and benefit my parents. So, if all of us are to be filial [children], can we set about it any other way than by first making a point of loving and benefiting other [people's] parents?"[3]

Mozi's point is that everyone will be better off if we all follow a practice of universal, impartial love. It's worth noting that Mozi is not saying that universal love is intrinsically good. It is, instead, a *means* for bringing about the good. This is what makes it consequentialist. As he explains:

Now if we seek to benefit the world by taking universality as our standard, those with sharp ears and clear eyes will see and hear for others, those with sturdy limbs will work for others.... Those who are old and without [family] will find means of support and be able to live out their days; the young and orphaned who have no parents will find someone to care for them and look after their needs.[4]

This passage suggests the benefits that Mohists sought to advance—namely, life, wealth, and social order—and the harms they wished to avoid—namely, death, poverty, and disorder or conflict.[5] Although we might disagree about the goals that Mohists value, the important point here is that in order to assess what we should do they direct us to look at the consequences for society as a whole. If the members of our society work to maximize the right social goods, then the benefits will flow to them individually.

Stop and Think

What are some other good consequences for society as a whole that a contemporary Mohist might pursue?

3.2   Utilitarianism

In the eighteenth century an English philosopher, Jeremy Bentham, developed a similar idea, which he dubbed **utilitarianism**. Bentham was scientifically minded, which one can see in the way he approached ethics. He posited that we all pursue pleasure and avoid pain. This provided him with what he called a **principle of utility**, which is, in effect, a theory of the good. In brief, Bentham thought it is good to maximize pleasure and minimize pain.[6]

He suggested we should do a kind of calculus when we are trying to figure out what will maximize utility. We should identify the likely outcomes of different possible courses of action, consider who is affected, and estimate the intensity, duration, and immediacy of the pleasures and pains that would be produced for each individual under each scenario, as well as our degree of certainty in these outcomes.[7] As with Mohism, everyone counts equally. We are not allowed to weigh our own pleasures and pains more heavily in this calculation.

While this view is often identified with the slogan "the greatest good for the greatest number," this isn't quite right. It is possible that one could achieve "the greatest good for the greatest number" by inflicting so much misery on a small group of people that the total utility is less than an alternative that brings less good to fewer people but suffering to none. The utilitarian calculus requires us to account for the total sum of positive utility (for Bentham, pleasure) *and* negative utility (for Bentham, pain) for each possible course of action and weigh these sums against each other.

Later thinkers have modified utilitarianism in various ways. Some have argued that the principle of utility needs revision, suggesting that happiness and suffering are much richer and more morally nuanced ideas than mere pleasure and pain. This was the view of John Stuart Mill, another English thinker, who developed and refined Bentham's theory. Mill thought that many of the experiences that individuals value the most aren't those that simply bring them pleasure. Moreover, he thought that we might want to differentially rank pleasures. He famously wrote, "It is better to be a human being dissatisfied than a pig satisfied; better to be Socrates dissatisfied than a fool satisfied. And if the fool, or the pig, is of a different opinion, it is only because they only know their own side of the question."[8] Bentham likely would not have agreed. He remarked, "the question is not, *Can they reason?* or *Can they talk?* but *Can they suffer?*"[9] So, while both thinkers took the well-being of sentient nonhumans into account, they would have weighed them differently.

Some utilitarians have suggested that we need to consider something more easily countable than pleasures, pains, happiness, and suffering. Others have noted that we sometimes desire things that don't seem to involve any of these. They suggest that the principle of utility should focus on *preference satisfaction*. However, due to the tendency for humans to have wholly irrational preferences—for instance, frequently choosing to do things that harm them—other thinkers have suggested that we define utility in terms of the preferences that humans would have if we were perfectly (or sufficiently) rational beings. One can often see something like this approach in economics and rational decision theory.

3.2.1 Act Utilitarianism

While all utilitarians value consequences, they may differ in how they do this. One option is to employ a utilitarian calculus for each action. This approach, *act utilitarianism*, provides us with the following principle (quoting Boetzkes and Waluchow):

> An act is right if and only if there is no other action I could have done instead which either (a) would have produced a greater balance of utility over disutility; or (b) would have produced a smaller balance of disutility over utility.[10]

This is all a bit abstract, so it is useful to try it out in an imaginary scenario, using a classic utilitarian calculus.

Suppose you have the choice of three different actions (A, B, and C) and you reasonably believe that whichever you do will affect three different people (Xena, Yassar, and Zhu). You take into consideration the intensity, duration, immediacy, and degree of certainty of the positive and negative consequences of each possible action for each individual. On the basis of your principle of utility, you assign utility values to each person given each possible action. Then you just do the math, calculating the net utility for each action—this is the last column to the right in the table below.

Action	Xena's utility	Yassar's utility	Zhu's utility	Net Utility of the action
A	– 10	+ 3	+ 5	– 2
B	– 3	+ 2	+ 3	+ 2
C	+10	– 2	– 4	+ 4

Notice that even though action C makes two of three people worse off than any other possible action it is still the right thing to do because it has the greatest net utility. This *could* even be true if there were another possible action that had positive utility for everyone. (Suppose there were a fourth possible action, D, that had a value of +1 for each person. This would still only add up to +3 and thus provide less total utility than action C in this scenario.)

We can make this a little more tangible. Imagine you're Yassar and you own an apartment that you are currently renting to Xena. Xena lost her job a few months ago and, even with government assistance, she is now two months behind on rent. She is looking for a job but you don't expect she will be able to find one. Zhu is looking for an apartment and would like to rent the apartment that Xena currently occupies. Legally, you can evict Xena, but, as a committed act utilitarian, it's important to you that you do the morally right thing. You judge that you have three options: (A) you could evict Xena immediately and immediately rent the apartment to Zhu; (B) you could give Xena until the end of the month to find the money to pay her back rent and then evict her and rent it to Zhu if she fails (as you expect she will); or (C) you can just tell Xena that you are confident she will be able to pay her back rent eventually and tell Zhu that they will have to find another apartment.

Notice that even though it's the worst option for you (Yassar), action C is still the right thing to do. Even if Zhu was your best friend and Xena was the biggest jerk you'd ever met, if the calculus above is correct, option C is the right thing to do. Again, for utilitarians, all individuals count equally and all that matters is the net utility produced, whether we judge that in terms of pleasures (and pains), happiness (and suffering), or preferences. Also, notice how sensitive the consequences are to the situation of the individuals involved. It is easy to imagine all kinds of different circumstances that would influence the utility of each action for each individual, from whether Xena has other realistic living options, to Yassar's wealth, to Zhu's psychological capacity to deal with uncertainty, and so on.

Stop and Think

Are there any moral considerations in this situation that aren't captured if we just think about the consequences?

What are they?

There are several objections that people have raised to act utilitarianism. First, many people think that there are particular types of action or special relationships that matter, which are irrelevant from a utilitarian perspective. (We'll consider these ethical lenses in Chapter 4 and section 1 of Chapter 6, respectively.) For instance, suppose you have already promised the apartment to Zhu when you're trying to decide what to do. An act utilitarian will only value keeping this promise insofar as it affects the utility of the possible actions. To be sure, often breaking promises can cause the promise-breaker shame, anguish, and anxiety (disutility, on pretty much any principle of utility) and have real negative consequences for the person to whom the promise was made. However, if you have no scruples about breaking promises, Zhu's disutility isn't increased by the additional harm of having a promise broken, and there are no other adverse serial consequences, then breaking the promise is the best thing to do, according to an act utilitarian. Aside from possible consequences, the fact that you promised is ethically irrelevant. If we think that promises matter morally, then this appears to be a serious problem for this theory. Similarly, we may think that we have particular obligations to family and friends to watch out for their interests and that these cannot fully be captured simply by thinking about consequences in a totally impartial way.

A second objection concerns matters of equality. Action C in the table above significantly benefits one person, while the other two are significantly harmed. It has seemed to many that this sort of inequality counts against the rightness of the action that produces it. Maybe action B, which distributes utility more evenly than the other options, is better. It's not difficult to imagine cases in which considerations of equality run against other values. For instance, many people identify the vast inequalities of wealth, both within many nations and between nations, as fundamentally wrong, even if they maximize utility over all (though there is little reason to think they do). However, unless inequality itself has bad consequences for the individuals affected, a classical act utilitarian wouldn't consider it morally relevant. Indeed, it is not at all clear how the utilitarian method of assessing consequences—looking at the expected utility for each individual and then adding it all together—could address relational properties like equality, which depend on comparisons *between* the individuals affected. Notice that this is not a problem for the consequentialist lens as such, but a limitation of the aggregative approach of classical act utilitarianism. After all, a more Mohist approach, which focuses on benefitting society as a whole, could easily prioritize equality as a goal.

Another type of objection concerns matters of **justice**. Imagine the following scenario. Suppose you are a police superintendent in a town where a terrible violent crime has been committed and the perpetrator is still at large. The general populace of the community is not only terrified, but they are also very angry at what they consider to be the failure of the police and there are nightly protests that are getting increasingly violent. Although you have no leads, you do a utilitarian calculus where you consider framing one person for the crime. You reason as follows. If no arrest is made, thousands of people will suffer in the following ways: many people will continue to live in terror; the riots will continue and many people will be hurt, some even killed; many people's property will be damaged and some of their livelihoods ruined. If you frame a person who has no alibi, then these terrible consequences will be avoided. To be sure, one person will suffer terribly, but this is outweighed by the thousands of people who will be spared any disutility. If the numbers work out, this means that the right thing to do is to frame the innocent person. Also, notice that if you want to harm as few people as possible then you will target someone who is socially isolated and marginalized in the community, someone who likely already experiences significant forms of social injustice. Most people think this is clearly wrong. It is simply unjust to frame an innocent person and even worse if you choose them because they are oppressed. If you are not so sure, imagine that *you* are the innocent person who is framed—after all, utilitarianism is impartial.

Act utilitarianism faces another kind of challenge when we consider the **problem of free riders**. Imagine there is a water shortage in your town. The town council asks everyone to avoid watering their lawns (if they have them) and to take short showers only a few times a week. If most people do this, a catastrophic drought where there is not enough water to drink will be avoided. So, although everyone will experience some unpleasantness if they follow the council's recommendation, it is considerably less unpleasant than what would happen under drought conditions. Suppose you know that your neighbours are very civic-minded and are likely to comply with the order, which means there will be more than enough water saved to avoid the catastrophic drought. Then it doesn't really matter what you do, as the drought will be avoided. Indeed, because you will diminish your own utility by forgoing your two daily 20-minute showers (you don't have a lawn) and because the right thing to do is to maximize utility, it seems you are morally obliged to keep up your high consumption of water, according to act utilitarianism. The cost in utility to others in the community would be zero, or negligibly small.[11] If people were to find out that you're a free rider this might make them angry (an unpleasant emotion that diminishes their happiness), or they might start acting the way you do, risking a drought. So to maximize the overall utility you should cover up and lie about your own water consumption. It seems, once again, that an act utilitarian approach is requiring one to behave in ways that are fundamentally unfair and immoral.

Stop and Think

Might similar objections be raised against Mohism?

After all, Mohists argue against focusing on personal relationships.

Might the pursuit of Mohist goals lead to injustice against individuals and problems with free riders?

3.2.2 Rule Utilitarianism

Prompted by such concerns, some have proposed a rule-based approach to utilitarianism, *rule utilitarianism*. The basic idea is that we need to identify those rules that, if everybody followed them, would maximize utility. Thus, we get a principle like the following (quoting Boetzkes and Waluchow):

> An act is morally right if and only if it conforms with a set of rules whose general observance would maximize utility.[12]

At least initially, this version of utilitarianism seems able to address all three of the challenges to act utilitarianism outlined above. Obviously, it deals with the free rider problem, but it also seems to deal with the scenario where an innocent person is framed for a crime. We considered the utility of only one framing; but if this were the *rule* for law enforcement, the result would be considerable disutility, terrorizing the innocent and ignoring real criminals, letting crime escalate. As for questions of equality, rule utilitarianism at least promises to treat like cases alike. Thus it conforms to formal justice, which is a significant step towards equal treatment (though not, perhaps, more nuanced views of equity). Rule utilitarianism also seem to fare better considering special relationships. For example, even though in some cases parents taking special care of their children might produce lower utility, if every parent followed the rule that parents should take special care of their children this would probably maximize utility.

However, some critics have complained that rule utilitarianism gives up much of what was really useful about the act utilitarian perspective. Consequentialism allows us to consider all the nuances and details of a particular situation. When we use the same set of rules to apply to a wide variety of situations, we may lose some valuable flexibility.

3.3   Final Considerations about Approaches that Focus on Consequences

While there are significant similarities between Mozi's consequentialism and utilitarianism there are also some differences. Perhaps the most significant similarity, beyond consequentialism itself, is that they both emphasize impartiality—that one shouldn't value one's own well-being (or that of those close to us) more than anybody else's. This means that Mohism and utilitarianism suggest that everyone who counts enjoys equal moral status. The key difference is in what these theories value and how they think of the collective. Utilitarians think of the collective simply as the sum of individuals; you determine utility for relevant individual and then add it all up. Mozi values wealth, social order, and community growth as properties of the collective. Consider social order. This is not the property of an individual and so it is not a possible principle of utility. Mozi can directly value social order in his system because the consequences he wants to bring about are the good of society as a whole, not the good of society understood as a collection of individuals.

Stop and Think

What are the different strengths and weaknesses of the different theories that focus on consequences?

Do you think one is better than the others?

Importantly for applied ethics, harm/benefit analyses invariably take up a kind of consequentialist lens. After all, harms are typically nothing other than bad consequences and benefits are typically good consequences. The challenge with harm/benefit analyses, just as with consequentialism more generally, is figuring out what counts—pleasure, happiness, preferences, social order, life, wealth—who counts—only humans or some nonhuman animals (and, perhaps, other nonhuman entities) too—and how to weigh what are often very different kinds of consequences against each other.

Chapter 3 Quiz

1. True or False: Utilitarians and Mohists agree that people need to be less partial when making moral decisions—no person should be prioritized over another.

2. True or False: Utilitarians just believe we should try to create the greatest good for the greatest number.

3. True or False: As explained above, Mozi defends the importance of impartiality on the basis that humans are really all just the same. It's not that partiality leads to bad consequences but just that it is illogical.

4 True or False: Rule utilitarianism states that we use the basic principles of utilitarianism to determine a set of rules that, when followed, would often maximize utility.

Further Reading

In addition to the sources in the endnotes, the following may be helpful:

Consequentialism
Shaw, William. "The Consequentialist Perspective." In *Contemporary Debates in Moral Theory*, edited by James Drier, 5–20. Malden: Blackwell Publishing, 2006.

Mohism
Lyceum of Philosophy. "MOZI: World's 1st Utilitarian & OG Minimalist Philosopher: An Introduction." YouTube. May 24, 2020. Video. https://www.youtube.com/watch?v=Yp9ovoxeUsg.

Van Norden, Bryan W. *Virtue Ethics and Consequentialism in Early Chinese Philosophy*. Cambridge: Cambridge University Press, 2007. See Part 3: "Mozi and Early Mohism."

Wong, David. "Chinese Ethics." In *The Stanford Encyclopedia of Philosophy* (Summer 2021 Edition), edited by Edward N. Zalta, last modified September 14, 2018, §3. https://plato.stanford.edu/archives/sum2021/entries/ethics-chinese.

Utilitarianism
Driver, Julia. *Consequentialism*. London: Routledge, 2012.

Mason, Elinor. "Consequentialism, Blame, and Moral Responsibility." In *The Oxford Handbook of Consequentialism*, edited by Douglas W. Portmore, 162–78. Oxford: Oxford University Press, 2020. https://doi.org/10.1093/oxfordhb/9780190905323.001.0001.

Smart, J.J.C. "Extreme and Restricted Utilitarianism." *Philosophical Quarterly* 6 (1956): 344–54.

Warburton, Nigel, and Philip Schofield. "Philip Schofield on Jeremy Bentham's Utilitarianism." Produced by the Institute of Philosophy. *Philosophy Bites*. February 11, 2012. Podcast. https://philosophybites.com/2012/02/philip-schofield-on-jeremy-benthams-utilitarianism.html.

The above links are available at:

sites.broadviewpress.com/ethicsprimer/chapter-3

4
Focus on Action (and Duty)

The next approach that we are going to consider focuses on actions and their motivations and whether they are right or wrong. The idea is that we have certain duties—actions that we must do—whether because of our social role, because of obligations incurred by past actions, or simply because they are the right things to do. The rightness of an action is determined by the kind of action it is and the motive behind it.

People often contrast this kind of approach—called deontology or duty ethics—with consequentialism. **Deontology** emphasizes the intrinsic rightness of an action regardless of any consequences, while consequentialism favours bringing about the best ends regardless of the actions required to do so. Realistically, this is a bit of an oversimplification, but this kind of cartoon can help one get a grip on the basic idea before adding more nuance.

Many people think that both approaches are valuable. Consistent with the ethical lens idea, applied ethicists often articulate basic principles at least one of which is deontological and another of which is consequentialist. For instance, bioethicists often emphasize that physicians should do no harm—a consequentialist goal—but also have a duty to inform their patients about their condition and available treatments—a deontological commitment. Similarly, research ethics requires that researchers honestly represent their results—a deontological commitment—and also demands that researchers care for the well-being of their participants/subjects—a consequentialist commitment. Because these are fundamentally different ethical orientations, they can conflict. When they do, this is often a sign that an ethical issue is particularly challenging.

One of the tricky things about duties is figuring out how we acquire them and who has which duties. As noted, there are different deontological approaches identifying different sources of our duties. Although the three approaches below are not meant to be exhaustive, they capture common ways of thinking about duties.

4.1   Duties Based on Roles

We begin with the idea that specific social roles come with particular duties. A famous passage from the *Bhagavad Gita*, one of the central texts in Hinduism, touches on this approach to duty. (The *Gita* certainly does much more than this—it is one of the great texts of world literature and broaches multiple fundamental philosophical issues. Here, we merely brush the surface of one of the many important themes in this work.) The *Gita* recounts part of a story about the moral struggles of Arjuna, a prince and hero who must fight a battle against his cousins. Arjuna is full of doubt and grief at the idea of killing his kin, and the destruction of war more generally, but is nonetheless bound by his duty as a warrior and the justness of his cause to take up arms. He asks his charioteer, Krishna, who is (unbeknownst to Arjuna) an avatar of Lord Vishnu, what he should do.

We can see Arjuna struggling with two competing duties based on kinds of social role. First, there is the duty not to kill his kin, the duty he has as a family member. Second, there is his duty as a prince and warrior to save his people from the unjust rule of his cousins. Horrified by the thought of killing so many, particularly friends and family, Arjuna resolves not to fight. Krishna admonishes Arjuna and urges him to change his mind. Among the various arguments that Krishna offers, the one that interests us has to do with Arjuna's social role. Krishna points out that for a warrior there is no higher purpose than a just war. For a warrior, to refuse to fight is to abandon one's duty.[1] The role of warrior has within it a duty to fight.

The idea that many professions come with specific duties is especially pertinent for applied ethics. For instance, a physician has particular duties concerning protecting and promoting the health and well-being of their patients and an engineer has particular duties to produce designs that fulfill their functions. Many professions come with **fiduciary obligations**. These are duties that come from particular relations of trust constraining how a professional can act on behalf of their client. For instance, lawyers have fiduciary obligations to act in their clients' interests and as directed by their clients. Although some professional fiduciary obligations are somewhat nebulous and vague, others are stipulated and enforced by professional societies or enshrined in law. So, for example, lawyers failing in their fiduciary obligations may be disciplined or disbarred by the relevant law society. The key idea for us is that certain kinds of professions or social roles come with duties that are particular to those roles.

Stop and Think

What is your ideal job?

Are there particular duties that someone in that profession has because of the nature of the profession?

(Note, not all professions or social roles have these kinds of particular duties, so it's important to notice which ones do.)

4.2 Duties Based on Past Actions

Another approach to deontology recognizes that some of our current duties rest on our past actions and the past actions of others—an idea explored by twentieth-century English thinker, W.D. Ross. Consequentialism is limited, Ross thought, because it only concerns itself with the future, not acknowledging the important role of the past in determining what we should do. For instance, Ross suggests that we acquire particular duties when we make promises. As a tangible example, at this moment, Letitia doesn't have a duty to pick up Clarisse at the airport. However, if Letitia had promised Clarisse that she would do so, then she would have acquired the duty to keep this promise and pick up Clarisse at the airport. Letitia is doing something wrong if she doesn't do as she promised. The same action—not picking up Clarisse— would not count as a wrong if Letitia never made the promise.

We can also acquire duties from committing harm. Suppose Letitia had promised to pick up Clarisse at the airport and failed to do so. We might think that Letitia has, at the very least, a duty to apologize. If Letitia's negligence led to significant harm—maybe Clarisse had to spend the night at the airport—Letitia acquires a duty to try to ameliorate the harm or correct it. If Letitia frequently picks up Clarisse from the airport, we might think that Clarisse acquires a duty too. We would expect her to show gratitude and perhaps reciprocate in some way.

Ross identified three types of duty that come from past actions that fit those described in the above scenarios—duties of fidelity, reparation and gratitude. **Duties of fidelity** are duties to be trustworthy and keep our promises. **Duties of reparation** come into effect when we have harmed or wronged someone. They are duties to repair a situation or otherwise make amends. **Duties of gratitude** arise when others help or support us. Through their actions, we acquire a duty to reciprocate or, at least, be grateful for their benefitting us.[2] Ross did not suggest that these duties exhaust all the possible types of duty. Indeed, he also suggested we have forward-looking duties of **non-maleficence** (not harming others), **beneficence** (improving the well-being of others), self-improvement, and **justice**.

Another useful idea Ross offers is that duties are often *prima facie*. *Prima facie* simply means "at first glance." An act which is a *prima facie duty*, then, is required *unless* there is some other competing duty that outweighs it in moral force.[3] It's easy to see—when we consider Ross's list of duties—why he needs an idea like this. After all, there are many situations where these duties may compete. Think back to the scenario with Xena, Yassar, and Zhu (section 3.2.1) and put yourself in Xena's shoes. On the one hand, Xena has the duty of fidelity, which means she should keep the promise to pay her rent, which is likely explicit in her lease (but would be implicit in renting even without a lease). On the other hand, we may think that her duty to protect her own interests, personal security, and well-being, implied by the duty of self-improvement, means she should try to convince Yassar to let her stay in the apartment, even if she can't pay her rent.

How is one to decide between competing duties? Ross, unfortunately, offers little help on this matter. However, if we treat ethical theories as lenses that help us appreciate the moral contours of ethical life, we might find that other ethical theories can help us weigh these various duties.

4.3 Duties Based on Reason Alone— The Categorical Imperative

A particularly influential deontological approach was first articulated by the eighteenth-century German philosopher, Immanuel Kant. Kant believed that we could figure out what our duties are on the basis of reason alone. He called the principle that grounds our duties the **Categorical Imperative**.

The Categorical Imperative is a fundamental principle of human choice and action that defines our moral obligations. Kant thought that this is, in effect, hard-wired into the rational part of our minds and we can discover it and make it explicit to ourselves to better guide our actions. The Categorical

Imperative entails a set of duties, or moral laws, specifying actions that are intrinsically right or wrong—that is, that are (he supposed) always right or wrong, in themselves, regardless of circumstances or consequences.

Kant recognized that there may be instances where we do what appears to be the morally right thing but only because it will benefit us or bring about some other desired end. For example, consider a millionaire who donates a proportion of their wealth to charity but only because they get a tax break. While this seems like a good thing to do because it benefits a worthy cause, Kant would argue that the action isn't praiseworthy because it is done for the wrong reasons. The millionaire's goal is to get a tax break. They are acting for selfish reasons. For Kant, even though it brings about good consequences, the act itself lacks moral worth. To act in accordance with the Categorical Imperative, one must act the right way for the right reasons.[4] It is just something you must do. This moral law is exceptionless, rather like a natural law.

The problem is, how do you discover, let alone justify, these duties? Kant was impressed by the fact that most humans are both free and rational. He thought that we can use our rational capacities to identify the Categorical Imperative and then freely choose to follow the moral law and the duties that flow from it. So, he proposed a kind of rational test, commonly referred to as the **Formula of Universal Law**. He suggested that when considering an action, we should articulate the **maxim** that describes that action—basically, the rule we would be following were we to act in this way.[5] Then we should ask ourselves, could we will that the maxim be a universal law, akin to a natural law (like universal gravitation or $E=mc^2$). In other words, could we rationally will that everyone would always act according to this maxim? If not, we shouldn't do it. Kant's test (at least at its best) is a logical one. The question is about whether it is *logically* possible to will the maxim as a universal law.

Kant considers the following:

> Let the question be, for example: May I when in distress make a promise with the intention not to keep it? ... [T]o discover the answer to this question ... [I] ask myself, "Should I be content that my maxim (to extricate myself from difficulty by a false promise) should hold good as a universal law, for myself as well as for others?" and should I be able to say to myself, "Everyone may make a deceitful promise when they find themselves in a difficulty from which they cannot otherwise extricate themselves?" Then I presently become aware that while I can will the lie, I can by no means will that lying should be a universal law. For with such a law there would be no promises at all, since it would be in vain to allege my

intention in regard to my future actions to those who would not believe this allegation, or if they over hastily did so would pay me back in my own coin. Hence my maxim, as soon as it should be made a universal law, would necessarily destroy itself.[6]

Thus, according to Kant, the wrongness of deceitfully promising can be appreciated through the fact that it is impossible to consistently will it. The same reasoning applies to lying more generally. A world where people always lied would be one in which people could never succeed in telling a lie. Lying only works because there is an expectation that people tell the truth. If we cannot will that everyone follows the maxim that we are considering following ourselves, that reveals our duty to follow a different course of action. So, in this case, the impossibility of willing that everyone should lie all the time grounds our duty to tell the truth.

The lying example also illustrates another formulation of Kant's Categorical Imperative, sometimes called the **Formula of Humanity**.[7] It states, "*So act that you use humanity, as much in your own person as in the person of every other, always at the same time as an end and never merely as a means.*"[8] To understand this (and why Kant thought this is another formulation of the same idea) you first need to know why Kant thought rationality and freedom are so important to morality.

Kant believed that the ability to rationally decide and then freely act was characteristic of moral beings. It is these capacities that allow us to plan our lives and pursue our goals. Indeed, it is the ability to reason, and so recognize through careful reflection our duties, as well as our freedom to act according to these duties, that constitute morality. This capacity for self-governance is called **autonomy**. Autonomous beings are capable of overcoming their inclinations and emotions. They are not simply driven by psychological or biological processes; they can *choose* to act on the basis of *reason* (or not).

Autonomy, thought Kant, gives beings special moral status—they are "ends in themselves." This is a way of saying that autonomous beings have moral status not because of some other goal, consequence, or value. They have inherent moral worth *because* they can act for their own reasons. As such, Kant believed it is wrong to treat any free and rational being merely as a means to achieving some goal or end. Insofar as we are autonomous, we are moral equals, and we cannot justify valuing ourselves over anyone else. Violating someone's autonomy—treating one's self or another person as if they are neither rational nor worthy of equal moral consideration—is one of the worst things you can do to an autonomous being. This idea, often called **respect for persons**, has been extremely important in philosophy in the

European tradition and, arguably, grounds the idea of universal human rights (which we will return to in Chapter 9).

We have already considered how lying violates the Formula of Universal Law, but we can now see how it also violates the Formula of Humanity. After all, lying violates the other person's autonomy. If you lie in order to further your own ends, you are treating those you deceive merely as a means to fulfilling your goals. After all, presumably, you are lying to them because you believe that if you told them the truth, they wouldn't act the way you want them to. By limiting their access to the truth, you are diminishing their capacity to make rational decisions; and by trying to manipulate their behaviour you are limiting their freedom. Deceiving someone is a way of using them for your own ends and preventing them from choosing their own.

Despite the importance of Kant in the legal, political, and ethical traditions of Europe and European settler societies, there are some serious concerns with this approach. First, remember that it's the maxim of an action that must pass the Universal Law test; but it's not entirely clear how to come up with the relevant maxim. Typically, any given action can be described in a variety of ways and so there are several different maxims that might be used to capture a given act. Suppose you are in the position of the person considering the lying promise, described above. However, the reason you are considering lying is because it is the only way you can get some money and, without this money, you will be unable to feed your children and they will starve. So you consider this maxim: "When someone's child is threatened with death, they must do whatever it takes to save them." It seems reasonable to think that you can will this as a universal law. The question is, which maxim is the right one to use when you are considering what you should do: the maxim that says lie and break a promise, or the one that says do whatever you must to save your children?

Although the challenge of articulating the right maxim stands, Kant has a clear reply in this particular case. Any time you lie or break a promise you are doing something wrong because the action violates the Formula of Humanity; you are failing to respect another person's autonomy, which means that you fail to respect their inherent worth as a person. In the imagined scenario, when you lie to someone, even in order to save your child, you are taking away that person's freedom to use their own rationality to think through what they should do and help you. If there is a good reason for you to get the money, despite not having the capacity or intention to pay it back, then, as a rational and free being, they are capable of recognizing that too. If you lie to them, you don't respect them. You are just treating them as a means to getting money and not an end in themselves.

Summary of the Formulations of Kant's Categorical Imperative

The **Categorical Imperative** commands our reason and requires us to act according to the moral law, irrespective of our desires and interests. We have looked at two formulations of the Categorical Imperative:

- The **Formula of Universal Law**: one must be able to universalize the maxim on which you intend to act without any contradiction.

- The **Formula of Humanity**: one may never disrespect a person's autonomy by treating them merely as a means to an end, but must treat all people as ends in themselves.

4.4   Final Considerations about Approaches that Focus on Action

While Kantian ethics has dominated discussions of deontology over the last few hundred years in societies that are shaped by the European tradition, it is worth remembering that the idea that we have basic duties is global and ancient. Whether duties are categorical, or are specific to social role, or acquired through previous actions, the view that some types of action are morally required and that the motivations behind actions matter ethically is common.

While both consequentialism and deontology are particularly adept at addressing moral problems when they arise, virtue ethics and relational ethics are more oriented to how to live life well or what makes a good life as a whole. It is to these rather different ways of approaching ethics that we now turn.

Chapter 4 Quiz

1. True or False: A fiduciary obligation refers to any duty that one has due to a social role.

2. Fill in the missing words: W.D. Ross argues that a _____ duty is required until it is outweighed by another, stronger moral duty.

3. Why is rationality important in Kant's moral theory?
    a. Since human beings are rational, we have the capacity to decide what is moral or not, and then decide to act morally.

    b.   All rational beings deserve equal respect and consideration when deciding how one should act morally.

    c.   Since human beings are rational, we must consider the ends of all of our actions but not the means by which we perform them when deciding how one should act morally.

    d.   a and b.

    e.   b and c.

    f.   All three of a, b, and c.

4.   According to Kant, the moral worth of an action depends on:

    a.   the moral character of the agent who performs the action

    b.   the consequences of the action (the end, not the means)

    c.   moral duties that we have to follow despite other goals we might have

5.   True or False: The Kantian idea of respect for persons is the idea that all humans matter just because they're a member of the species *Homo sapiens*.

Further Reading

In addition to the sources in the endnotes, the following may be helpful:

On Duty in General

Warburton, Nigel, and David Owens. "David Owens on Duty." Produced by the Institute of Philosophy. *Philosophy Bites*. September 1, 2015. Podcast. https://philosophybites.libsyn.com/david-owens-on-duty.

Duties Based on Roles

Flood, Gavin, and Charles Martin, translators. *The Bhagavad Gita: A New Translation*. New York: W.W. Norton and Company, 2012.

Gupta, Bina. "'Bhagavad Gītā' as Duty and Virtue Ethics: Some Reflections." *The Journal of Religious Ethics* 34, no. 3 (September 2006): 373–95. https://www.jstor.org/stable/40017693.

Hinrichs, Allison. "The Bhagavad-Gita: Righteousness or Duty?" *The Spectator*, March 15, 2022. https://www.spectatornews.com/opinion/2022/03/the-bhagavad-gita-righteousness-or-duty/.

Duties Based on Past Action

Atwell, John. "Ross and Prima Facie Duties." *Ethics* 88, no. 3 (April 1978): 240–49. https://www.jstor.org/stable/2379943.

Robinson, Michael. "Are Some Prima Facie Duties More Binding Than Others?" *Utilitas* 22, no. 1 (February 2010): 26–32. https://doi.org/10.1017/S0953820809990343.

Duties Based on Reason Alone

CrashCourse. "Kant & Categorical Imperatives: Crash Course Philosophy #35." YouTube. November 14, 2016. Video. https://www.youtube.com/watch?v=8bIys6JoEDw.

Johnson, Robert, and Adam Cureton. "Kant's Moral Philosophy." In *The Stanford Encyclopedia of Philosophy* (Fall 2020 Edition), edited by Edward N. Zalta, last modified July 7, 2016. https://plato.stanford.edu/archives/fall2020/entries/kant-moral/.

Korsgaard, Christine M. "Kant's Formula of Universal Law." *Pacific Philosophical Quarterly* 66, no. 1–2 (1985): 24–47. https://doi.org/10.1111/j.1468-0114.1985.tb00240.x.

O'Neill, Onora. *Acting on Principle: An Essay on Kantian Ethics*. 2nd ed. Cambridge: Cambridge University Press, 2013. https://doi.org/10.1017/CBO9781139565097.

The above links are available at:

sites.broadviewpress.com/ethicsprimer/chapter-4

5
Focus on Character (and Virtues)

While acting in the right way and bringing about good consequences matter for the ethical theories we discuss in this chapter, their central focus is on developing virtues, avoiding vices, living well, and being a good person. The idea is that if one has the right kind of character, developing one's virtues and correcting one's vices, then one will, as a result of this, do the right things and good consequences will follow. As with consequentialism and deontology, we can find versions of this approach, often called virtue ethics, in many different cultural traditions.

Although philosophers have different ways of identifying virtues and characterizing the good life, most virtue ethics approaches recognize that developing a good character takes practice. The disposition to be good is, in effect, a habit of behaving well. Good habits are typically acquired by repetition, whether we repeat these actions mindfully or simply by inclination; just as bad habits are acquired by repeatedly behaving badly. Thus, many virtue ethicists emphasize the importance of education or having a social environment that supports the acquisition of virtue as well as discussing how those of us who want to be better people can shape our own characters. Often, when someone tells a story about an exemplary person with the clear implication that others ought to act the same way, they are engaged in a kind of virtue ethics.

5.1   The Good Life, According to Aristotle

The most famous virtue ethicist in the European tradition is Aristotle (384–322 BCE). His book, *The Nicomachean Ethics*, begins by identifying the good as that which people pursue for its own sake. While we can see that many people pursue things like pleasure and wealth, these are not the kinds of ends that Aristotle has in mind. After all, wealth is only an *instrumental good* as it merely provides a means for obtaining things that we hope will make us happy but does not provide happiness directly (or particularly reliably). Similarly, pleasure is often a sign of the good—particularly for virtuous people who take pleasure in acting virtuously—but it is not itself good. Aristotle believed that what we pursue is *happiness* and a happy life is the ultimate good that humans seek. Although we have used the term "happiness," this isn't a perfect translation. The Greek term Aristotle used is "**eudaemonia**," which is variously translated as happiness, flourishing, and well-being.[1]

It is important to understand that Aristotle is not just saying that if you behave virtuously, then you will experience happiness. *Eudaemonia* is nothing other than living virtuously, functioning well as a human being over a continuous period of time by consistently doing the right thing. (This is one of the reasons why many translators prefer the term "flourishing" as a translation of *eudaemonia*.)

From *eudaemonia*, positive and appropriate emotions flow. Emotional responses, like virtuous character traits, are acquired through habit and, though they should not override reason, Aristotle believed they had an important role in our moral lives.

Aristotle had a very particular account of the virtues, each one of which he thought was situated between two vices—one of excess and the other of deficiency. So, for instance, Aristotle thought that the virtue of courage is a middle way between the vices of cowardice and recklessness.[2] He has a long list of virtues with their attendant vices, and even with its length, there is little reason to think his list is exhaustive.

Although we may wonder if this account of virtue accurately captures the character of all virtues and vices, careful consideration of some cases shows its usefulness. One of the virtues Aristotle considers is *proper pride*, what we might think of as appropriate self-regard. Someone with proper pride thinks themselves worthy and is worthy; they make claims to appropriate treatment by others in accord with their merits. Thus, Aristotle notes, proper pride is a kind of "crown of the virtues"[3] as one must have already achieved great things to properly feel it. This virtue sits between the excess of *vanity*, where one believes that they deserve more than they truly merit, and a vice of *false modesty* or inappropriate humility. Both of these vices reflect a failure to accurately appreciate one's own merits. Such failures may lead one to act badly because one has over-estimated one's capacities, in the case of the vanity, or fail to act at all, as in the case of the inappropriate humility.

Similarly, anger can be virtuous or vicious. Aristotle identifies the good-tempered person as someone "who gets angry at the right things and with the right people, and also in the right way and at the right time and for the right length of time."[4] Being good-tempered rests between the vices of being hot-tempered—where one easily angers, directs one's anger at the wrong targets, or is sulky or vengeful—and a deficiency where one doesn't care about anything at all or is willing to accept abuse of oneself or others.

Stop and Think

We have mentioned three virtues—proper pride, courage, and being good tempered—and how they are each situated between two vices—one of deficiency and one of excess.

What are some other examples of virtues and their concomitant vices?

Are there any virtues that aren't situated as a mean between two vices?

The thing to notice in these examples is that there isn't a rule that will tell you how to be courageous, how to have proper pride, or how to feel and express appropriate anger. Nor is there an ordering of virtues and vices that tells you which virtues are more important than others. Indeed, the appropriate action in any given situation is often particular to that situation. What we can say is that the virtuous person will act well no matter the situation and will, by so doing, flourish and live a successful, happy life.

Critics have complained that, without more specific guidance, Aristotelian ethics is of little use when it comes to solving moral dilemmas. To implore us to do what's virtuous doesn't help us assess what exactly that is. After all, unless we have more to go on, we might choose people with terrible character flaws as our moral exemplars and cultivate vices while thinking that we are following a life of virtue. Similarly, being told that a virtuous character is one that avoids too much and too little of anything seems like empty advice. Aristotle does not provide recipes or calculations for virtue. He assumes that what constitutes the virtuous life is an objective matter, rooted in human nature, and that we can recognize it when it appears in ourselves or others.

5.2 The Good Life, According to Buddhism

Though it is a controversial reading, a number of contemporary thinkers treat Buddhist ethics as a type of virtue ethics. One of the complications here is that even if we concede that much of Buddhist ethics addresses the acquisition of virtuous ways of thinking and acting, it starts with a big dose of consequentialism. Like Aristotle's ethics, Buddhist ethics begins with an observation about human lives. Indeed, this insight about the nature of life is Buddhism's First Noble Truth: **dukkha**—which is translated as "dissatisfaction" or "dis-ease," and (more controversially) "suffering"—is an inescapable part of life. The Buddha is thought to have said:

> ... [B]irth is suffering; aging is suffering; sickness is suffering; death is
> suffering; sorrow and lamentation, pain, grief and despair are suffer-
> ing; association with the unpleasant is suffering; dissociation from
> the pleasant is suffering; not to get what one wants is suffering ...[5]

Having recognized this, the aim of Buddhism is really about figuring out how to live so as to minimize *dukkha*—clearly a consequentialist goal.

However, the guidance that Buddhism gives for achieving this goal focuses on the cultivation of ways of thinking and behaving that fit the model of virtue ethics. For instance, the Second Noble Truth identifies the source of *dukkha* as what are, in effect, vices. The central vice identified here is *attachment*. Attachment includes things like greed and lust but more gener-ally refers to craving or desire for things. Along with attachment, ignorance and hatred constitute the "three poisons" that tend to give rise to *dukkha*. So, dispositions to dismiss or be indifferent to the truth, despise and harm oth-ers, or constantly acquire or desire more things are serious character flaws.

The Third Noble Truth just makes the obvious point that you can decrease *dukkha* by renouncing or rejecting what gives rise to it. In terms of the three poisons, instead of ignorance one should pursue wisdom, instead of hatred one should cultivate loving kindness, and instead of attachment, one should practice selflessness and generosity.

Stop and Think

In your own experience, can you think of a case where one of the three poisons—attachment, hatred, or ignorance—led you to behave badly?

Did your behaviour cause dissatisfaction, dis-ease, or suffering (for others or yourself)?

The Fourth Noble Truth further specifies the practices that the virtuous person should pursue to reduce *dukkha*—the Eightfold Path. These are, in effect, a basic guide to living well. While, for practicing Buddhists, this is part of a complex system of religious praxis, here we focus on the aspects of the Eightfold Path that are helpful for a secular ethics. Two parts focus on wisdom. The first is *right view*, which is the effort to gain the correct view of reality. The next is *right intention or thought*, which means (in part) cultivating compassion for all sentient beings. The next four focus on conduct. *Right speech* favours things like telling the truth over lying and slander, as well as speaking kindly and usefully rather than employing abusive language or engaging in gossip. *Right action* and *right livelihood* basically require you to find ways of living that don't promote *dukkha*, and *right effort* recognizes that this kind of virtuous conduct requires self-discipline. The final two parts of the Eightfold Path concern mental discipline. *Right mindfulness* requires cultivating an awareness of all one's activities and thoughts, while *right concentration* stills the mind and aids in the realization of peace and tranquility.[6]

5.3   The Exemplar of a Virtuous Person

Often virtue ethics approaches offer an ideal or exemplary person as a kind of role model to emulate. Similarly, we tell stories about vicious people to understand how their lives can go awry so that we do not make the same poor choices that they did. Such exemplars redirect ethics from the individual actions and moral dilemmas that are, typically, the focus of consequentialism and deontology to a more holistic way of thinking about a moral life.

Stop and Think

To you, who exemplifies a good person who is living well?

What are their virtues?

Can you recount a story about them that reveals their virtuous character?

Chapter 5 Quiz

1. Why is there an important consequentialist component of Buddhist ethics?
    a. Because Buddhism is centrally concerned with harm/benefit analyses.
    b. Because Buddhism is centrally concerned with the alleviation of dissatisfaction, dis-ease, and suffering.
    c. Because Buddhism is centrally concerned with creating a well-ordered society.
    d. Because Buddhism is centrally concerned with maximizing pleasure.

2. True or False: Aristotle believed that the ultimate goal of life is "*eudaemonia*," which is variously translated as "happiness," "flourishing," and "well-being."

3. True or False: Buddhism's First Noble Truth is that flourishing is crucial to human life.

4. Which of the following are part of Buddhism's Eightfold Path? Select all that apply.
    a. Right social structure—cultivating a society where the wealthiest people have the most power
    b. Right mindfulness—cultivating an awareness of all one's activities and thoughts
    c. Right duties—clearly expressing, on the basis of reason alone, the duties that all rational beings have and following those duties
    d. Right intention or thought—cultivating compassion for all sentient beings
    e. Right livelihood—making a living in ways that don't promote *dukkha*
    f. Right view—the effort to gain the correct view of reality

Further Reading

In addition to the sources in the endnotes, the following may be helpful:

The Good Life, According to Aristotle

Annas, Julia. "Being Virtuous and Doing the Right Thing." *Proceedings and Addresses of the American Philosophical Association* 78 (2004): 61–74.

Crash Course. "Aristotle & Virtue Theory: Crash Course Philosophy #38." YouTube. December 5, 2016. Video. https://www.youtube.com/watch?v=PrvtOWEXDIQ

Hursthouse, Rosalind. *On Virtue Ethics*. Oxford: Oxford University Press, 1999.
See esp. Chapters 1–3.

Warburton, Nigel, and Roger Crisp. "Roger Crisp on Virtue." *Philosophy Bites*. Produced by the Institute of Philosophy. October 12, 2008. Podcast. https://philosophybites.com/2008/10/roger-crisp-on.html.

The Good Life, According to Buddhism

Fink, Charles K. "Cultivation of Virtue in Buddhist Ethics." *Journal of Buddhist Ethics* 20 (2013). https://blogs.dickinson.edu/buddhistethics/2013/11/14/cultivation-of-virtue-in-buddhist-ethics/.

Garfield, Jay L. *Buddhist Ethics: A Philosophical Exploration*. Oxford: Oxford University Press, 2021.
See esp. Chapters 1, 2, 6, and 7 ("Methodological Introduction"; "The Broad Structure of Buddhist Ethics"; "The Four Noble Truths"; "Path as a Structure for Buddhist Ethics").

Keown, Damian. *Buddhist Ethics: A Very Short Introduction*. Oxford: Oxford University Press, 2005.
See esp. Chapter 1 ("Buddhist Morality") and Chapter 2 ("Ethics East and West").

Whitehill, James. "Buddhist Ethics as Virtue Ethics." *Journal of Buddhist Ethics* 1 (1994). https://blogs.dickinson.edu/ buddhistethics/2010/04/05/buddhist-ethics-in-western-context-the-virtues-approach/.

The above links are available at:

sites.broadviewpress.com/ethicsprimer/chapter-5

6

Focus on Relations

Whereas approaches that focus on character and virtue tend to consider how individuals can improve themselves, relational approaches begin from the idea that *nobody is truly self-made*. All relational ethics starts with particular views about who we are, how we live, and the nature of our psychology (and, indeed, biology) that emphasize relationality. The idea is we all are who we are through our relationships, so ethical decision-making needs to value and pay attention to them. Different traditions take different approaches to thinking about which relations create and constrain our moral lives.

We begin with feminist ethics, which was developed in reaction to the ethical traditions of Europe—especially utilitarianism (section 3.2) and Kantianism (section 4.3) and, to a lesser extent, Aristotelianism (section 5.1)—as well as the political discourse on rights that arose out of these theories (discussed below in Chapter 9). In the 1970s and 1980s, many feminists argued both that nobody is truly fully independent and, furthermore, that people vary significantly in their degree of personal and physical dependency on others, which informs what they can do and how they relate to other people. They also noted that social position and inequality shape people's lives and curtail their choices in ways that are ethically relevant. We are going to think about this first kind of relational ethics as focusing on personal relationships and this second kind as focusing on political relationships.

Then we turn to ethical approaches that foreground communal relations. These are less concerned with power than the kinds of relationships that we will consider under the moniker "political." This approach can be understood through the African idea of *ubuntu*, which places the community at the centre of moral decision-making. Finally, we will consider relational approaches that go beyond human relationships to all my relations, including those in the *more-than-human* world. This is an ethical framing that is common in traditional Indigenous value systems throughout what settlers call North America.

6.1   Focus on Personal Relationships

When feminist philosophers began to engage ethical theory in the 1970s, they noticed that the then dominant European approaches seemed to assume that the goal of ethics was to adjudicate conflicts and facilitate decision-making in the public sphere. By this, they meant that these theories only addressed issues that arose outside the home with parties who were mature, independent, impartial adults. The private sphere—i.e., home life, which is characterized by relationships of dependency and partiality—was simply ignored. The feminist critique was twofold. First, ethics needs to address the importance of personal relationships in our lives. Second, humans are, in fact, thoroughly relational beings and the idea that anyone is *self-made* is simply a myth. Minimally, all humans require huge amounts of care and education at the beginning of our lives if we are to develop into capable adults. Moreover, throughout our lives, we depend on others looking after us and helping us with various activities—from helping us secure work to addressing our most intimate personal needs. This doesn't mean merely that the kinds of relations we have with others are important causes of how we develop as persons. It also means that these kinds of relations constitute, in large part, who we are.

These ideas gave rise to a distinctive ethical approach called **care ethics**. Care ethics recognizes that relationships of care—for instance, parents caring for young children—cannot be captured by the ethical theories that have dominated European and European settler societies. After all, young children are not autonomous in a Kantian sense, as they do not have the capacity to reason, nor do they have the ability to overcome their inclinations. They are also extremely vulnerable; so, we may have special obligations to our own children because of their vulnerability and because we are in a unique and specific relationship of care with them. Perhaps most importantly of all, the ethical relationships that parents have with their children, indeed that all of us have with family members more generally, are *emotional* relationships. Caring for a child requires, not impartiality, but rather a thoroughly partial emotional investment in the life and well-being of the child. Love and care are not incidental to these relationships or a fortunate consequence of them; they are the very stuff of them.

A similar idea can also be found in ethics based on the work of Kongfuzi (or Confucian Ethics). **Confucianism** emphasizes that we learn how to be good people through our relationships with our family members, particularly our parents. We learn moral emotions, such as love, through loving our parents and siblings. The respect and love that we have for our parents is, in effect, the root for the love and respect that we show other people as adults. In this way, Confucians believe that our capacity for humaneness, our moral concern for humanity generally (*ren*, sometimes translated as human-heartedness[1]), emerges through our personal filial relationships.[2]

6.2   Focus on Political Relations

Although relational ethicists who focus on personal relationships often emphasize the positive ways in which these constitute us, it is important to remember that families can be places of inequality and various kinds of serious harms. Children are not only in need of care but are extraordinarily vulnerable to abuse and neglect. In patriarchal cultures, wives are often seen as subordinate to their husbands and have their freedom curtailed and their interests and needs overlooked or marginalized. Daughters are often similarly devalued.

These patriarchal views of women extend beyond the home. This makes it more difficult for women to leave abusive domestic situations and find better lives elsewhere because they are frequently seen as incompetent or incapable of filling any roles other than those traditionally assigned to women. Moreover, they may have internalized these patriarchal views so that they see themselves (and other women) as being properly subordinate to men and unfit for anything but traditional feminine roles. Such assumptions make it extremely difficult for women to succeed in various professions where they may be assumed to be deficient in virtues associated with men—such as rationality, morality, strength, and competence. Moreover, because traditional women's roles—including invaluable skilled care labour, such as growing or obtaining and cooking food, cleaning, and childcare—are devalued or characterized as essentially female, men often refuse to take on these roles, as they find them demeaning, or they lack the relevant skills. The feminist slogan **"the personal is political"** refers to the way in which inequality in our personal relationships scales up to produce inequality in our society and inequality in our society scales down and affects almost every aspect of our daily lives. "Political" in this sense isn't really about who you vote for but, in the words of a famous political theorist, "who gets what, when, how."[3]

Early feminist theories addressing the injustices of patriarchy were often criticized for only voicing the perspectives of straight, white, Anglo, settler, middle-class women without disabilities. Many of the women overlooked by these theories pointed out that they often experienced inequality quite differently. For instance, some suggested that poor women enjoyed greater equality with poor men than middle-class women did with middle-class men but greater inequality overall. Poor women did not long for access to the public sphere of work outside the home as they already worked outside the home, albeit often for wages significantly lower than men's wages. Many women maintained that much of the discrimination they faced had more to do with their racial or ethnic identity, their class, their sexuality, or their disability status than their gender. Moreover, not infrequently, this discrimination was enacted or exacerbated by more privileged women, some of whom claimed to be feminists.

US legal scholar, Kimberlé Crenshaw, coined the term **intersectionality** to capture this idea.[4] She recognized that in societies that have multiple axes of oppression—such as racism, colonialism, ableism, hetero- and cissexism, and classism—people who belong to more than one oppressed group often experience oppression in distinctive ways that are highly particular. These patterns of oppression can be difficult to predict and understand from the perspective of those who do not share similar social positionings and experiences.

Stop and Think

It's tempting to think of oppression as additive, so that the more oppressed groups you belong to the worse off you will be. But, as Crenshaw notes, this is not always true because the ways that social identities intersect are complicated.

Can you think of an example of intersectional identities where oppression (or privilege) isn't additive?

If we are committed to equality for all, we must pay attention to intersectional issues. This type of analysis highlights the fact that we are all located in complex webs of social power and privilege. While in an ideal world we might be able to treat everyone (outside our friends and family) impartially, in societies that are structured by patterns of injustice and inequality that disadvantage particular groups, we need to take the reality of these political relationships into account when we are making ethical decisions.

Because it is often difficult for those who are privileged in a certain respect to understand the true challenges and restrictions on those who aren't, it is particularly important to have people who experience oppression involved in decision-making about policies intended to address that oppression. Disability rights advocates coined the phrase **"nothing about us without us"**[5] to capture this idea. This is not only a call for inclusion but also a call to those allies who wish to support their cause to exercise humility—a warning that well-intentioned **paternalism** can actually exacerbate harms and inequality and undermine the autonomy of those whom one wishes to help. Understanding how the complex political relationships that we have with each other inform various ethical challenges and dilemmas is key to this relational approach to ethics.

6.3 · Focus on Communal Relations

While political approaches to relational ethics attend to the many social and political differences between us, communal approaches focus on the collective.

It is quite common in ethical theories outside the European tradition to focus more on the community than the individual (indeed, we have already seen a version of this with Mohism in section 3.1). The concept of **ubuntu** is a good example, as it rejects European individualism; it has been employed as a post-colonial ethical anchor for rebuilding more just communities and positive relationships in African societies recently freed from colonial oppression.[6] In South Africa's Truth and Reconciliation process—set up to document and deal with the appalling human rights abuses that happened under apartheid—*ubuntu* has been an important principle that has shaped how this process of restorative justice has been understood.[7]

Although, as South African jurist, Yvonne Mokgoro notes, *ubuntu* is not easily definable, particularly in a foreign tongue,[8] there are, nonetheless, a number of sayings and stories that point to the central idea. *The Report of the Truth and Reconciliation Commission* quotes Ms. Susan van der Merwe, whose husband was murdered in 1978:

The Tswanas have an idiom which I learned from my husband which goes "a person is a person by other people, a person is only a person with other people." We do have this duty to each other. The survival of our people in this country depends on our co-operation with each other. My plea to you is, help people throw their weapons away.... No person's life is a waste. Every person's life is too precious.[9]

Thus, *ubuntu* is associated with harmony and solidarity at the level of the group with processes aimed at adjudicating conflict focused on the restoration of peace in the community.[10] As Mokgoro notes:

> Group solidarity, conformity, compassion, respect, human dignity, humanistic orientation and collective unity have, among others been defined as key social values of *ubuntu*.... [I]ts value has also been viewed as a basis for a morality of co-operation, compassion, communalism and concern for the interests of the collective respect for the dignity of personhood, all the time emphasising the virtues of that dignity in social relationships and practices.[11]

Thus, *ubuntu* not only emphasizes a strong relational ethics that focuses on the community, it is also deeply humanist. *Ubuntu* recognizes that one's own humanity is inextricably bound with the humanity of others.

6.4   Focus on All My Relations

While the other three approaches in this chapter typically foreground different types of relationships between humans, the last includes these but goes beyond to consider relationships with the *more-than-human* world. This is the approach exemplified by the phrase **all my relations** that is central to the worldview and ethical orientation of many Indigenous peoples in what settlers have called North America. This perspective emphasizes not only the reality of our physical, psychological, and spiritual dependence on the many different beings in the world around us but also our capacity to affect these beings. For many Indigenous traditions, it is not only nonhuman animals who are included in these relations but plants and parts of the nonorganic world also.

Importantly, the relations acknowledged are not simply relations of interdependency but also relationships of respect. For instance, many traditional Mi'kmaw stories identify ways that plants and animals guide and teach humans. These stories recognize that nonhuman beings do not exist to serve humans but have their own moral status that demands respect.[12]

Failing to respect other beings can bring disastrous results to those humans who ignore their obligations to the more-than-human world. This ethical orientation brings with it gratitude to those beings who sustain our lives and a commitment to sustaining theirs. When one takes something from the world one should only take what is needed, which not only shows respect for what is taken but also ensures that there is plenty for others (human and nonhuman, alike). Reciprocity is often emphasized with the view that one should give back for the gifts that one receives. In this way, relationships remain mutually beneficial. Just as *ubuntu* emphasizes the value of harmony in the human community, all my relations emphasizes the value of harmony of humans with the many other beings in our world.

An adjacent idea in Indigenous cultures is the **seven generations** teaching. The seventh generation holds significance for many Indigenous peoples, such as the Anishinabek, Ojibway, and Haudenosaunee.[13] When thinking about what we should do, this teaching recommends that we consider the actions and traditions of the previous seven generations and the effect of our actions on the seven generations after us. The foundational principle of this teaching is that our choices, actions, and mistakes have a ripple effect throughout history. As Ojibway thinkers, Linda Clarkson, Vern Morrisette, and Gabriel Régallet explain:

> There is a teaching passed down from our ancestors that crystallizes our sense of responsibility and our relationship to the earth that arises out of the original law. It is said that we are placed on the earth (our Mother) to be the caretakers of all that is here. We are instructed to deal with the plants, animals, minerals, human beings and all life, as if they were a part of ourselves. Because we are a part of Creation, we cannot differentiate or separate ourselves from the rest of the earth. The way in which we interact with the earth, how we utilize the plants, animals and the mineral gifts, should be carried out with the seventh generation in mind. We cannot simply think of ourselves and our survival; each generation has a responsibility to "ensure the survival for the seventh generation."[14]

In considering our relation to the generations before us and the ones after us, the seven generations teaching emphasizes the connection with our ancestors and descendants. We live in a continuum, with each of us having parents, grandparents, and great grandparents (who, in turn, had parents, grandparents, and great grandparents), who we learn from and sometimes teach; and many of us have children, grandchildren, and great grandchildren (and some of them will have children, grandchildren, and great grandchildren), who we teach and learn from.[15] Some of us will spend time in every role. Everyone has a responsibility to learn from and teach past and present generations. Awareness of this interconnectedness within the community encourages one to act selflessly and sustainably for future generations.

Importantly, the seven generations teaching is not only forward looking, but it also emphasizes the importance of continuity with traditional and cultural origins. Failure to know and consider one's place in one's cultural history and traditions leads to alienation and an inability to understand one's own life. Knowing who you are and how you fit in the world is important for making ethical choices. Moreover, in knowing our history and traditions, we can avoid making the same mistakes as our ancestors. Such history and tradition should inform, guide, and support our present choices as we think about our impacts on future generations. We have a responsibility to bridge the gap between our past and future—by upholding and maintaining tradition, learning from our ancestors, and passing traditions to our descendants. The responsibility to all our relations is inherited from one's ancestors and passed onto future generations, solidifying one's bond with their community.

Stop and Think

Suppose we brought the seven generations teaching to our approaches that focus on consequences.

How would that change the way that we thought about the consequences of our possible actions?

Chapter 6 Quiz

1. True or False: Intersectionality is the idea that oppression is predictable and purely additive: the more oppressed groups one is a part of the more oppressed one will be, as one will experience all aspects of oppression associated with each oppressed group.

2. True or False: Confucians believe that the capacity for humaneness, our moral concern for humanity generally, emerges through our personal filial relationships.

3. True or False: The feminist critique of traditional ethics is twofold: ethics needs to address the importance of personal relationships in our lives; and humans are, in fact, thoroughly relational beings— the idea that anyone is self-made is simply a myth.

4. True or False: *Ubuntu* takes a communal approach that emphasizes the importance of relationships with nonhumans as well as humans; this is why *ubuntu* cannot be considered truly humanist.

5. True or False: "All my relations" simply refers to the other humans to whom one is related.

Further Reading

In addition to the sources in the endnotes, the following may be helpful:

Personal Relationships

Gilligan, Carol. *In a Different Voice*. Cambridge, MA: Harvard University Press, 1982.
    There is a nice excerpt of *In a Different Voice* in Russ Shafer-Landau, *Ethical Theory: An Anthology*, 2nd ed. (Hoboken, NJ: Wiley-Blackwell, 2012).

Noddings, Nell. "An Ethic of Caring." In *Caring: A Feminine Approach to Ethics and Moral Education*, 79–103. Berkeley: University of California Press, 1984.

Tao, Julia Po-Wah-Lai. "Two Perspectives of Care: Confucian Ren and Feminist Care." *Journal of Chinese Philosophy* 27, no. 2 (2000): 215–40.

Van Norden, Bryan W. *Virtue Ethics and Consequentialism in Early Chinese Philosophy*. Cambridge: Cambridge University Press, 2007.
    See Part 2 "Kongzi and Ruism."

Warburton, Nigel, and Aidan Turner. "Aidan Turner on Confucian Ancestor Worship." BBC. 2015. Video. https://www.bbc.co.uk/programmes/p02xbx9q.

Wong, David. "Chinese Ethics." In *The Stanford Encyclopedia of Philosophy* (Summer 2021 Edition), edited by Edward N. Zalta, last modified September 14, 2018. https://plato.stanford.edu/archives/sum2021/entries/ethics-chinese.
    See esp. §2.3–2.4.

Political Relations

Calhoun, Cheshire. "Justice, Care, and Gender Bias." *The Journal of Philosophy* 85, no. 9 (1988): 451–63. https://doi.org/10.2307/2026802.

Collins, Patricia Hills. *Intersectionality as Critical Social Theory*. London: Duke University Press, 2019.

Norlock, Kathryn. "Feminist Ethics." In *The Stanford Encyclopedia of Philosophy* (Summer 2019 Edition), edited by Edward N. Zalta, published May 27, 2019. https://plato.stanford.edu/archives/sum2019/entries/feminism-ethics.

Sherwin, Susan. "Ethics, 'Feminine' Ethics, and Feminist Ethics." In *No Longer Patient: Feminist Ethics and Health Care*, 35–57. Philadelphia: Temple University Press, 1992.

Communal Relations

Bell, Daniel A., and Thaddeus Metz. "Confucianism and *Ubuntu*: Reflections on a Dialogue between Chinese and African Traditions." *Journal of Chinese Philosophy* 38, no. 1 (2011): 78–95.

Masina, Nomonde. "Xhosa Practices of Ubuntu for South Africa." In *Traditional Cures for Modern Conflicts: African Conflict 'Medicine,'* edited by I. William Zartman, 169–81. Boulder: Lynne Rienner Publishers, 2000.

Metz, Thaddeus, and Joseph B.R. Gai. "The African Ethic of *Ubuntu/Botho*: Implications for Research on Morality." *Journal of Moral Education* 39, no. 3 (September 2010): 273–90. https://doi.org/10.1080/03057240.2010.497609.

Murove, Munyaradzi Felix, ed. *African Ethics: An Anthology of Comparative and Applied Ethics*. Scottsville: University of Kwazulu-Natal Press, 2009. Read esp. Part II Primacy of Ubuntu in African Ethics, Chapters 4–6.

All My Relations

Brant, Clare. "Native Ethics & Principles." Cape Breton University. 1982. https://www.cbu.ca/indigenous-affairs/mikmaq-resource-centre/mikmaq-resource-guide/essays/native-ethics-principles/.

"Episode #1: All My Relations & Indigenous Feminism." *All My Relations*. February 26, 2019. Podcast. https://www.allmyrelationspodcast.com/podcast/episode/32b0bd95 ep-1-all-my-relations-and-indigenous-feminism.

Government of Alberta. "All My Relations—Well-being." https://www.learnalberta.ca/content/aswt/well_being/documents/all_my_relations.pdf.

Native American History. "How Native Americans Made Decisions for the Future: 7 Generations Rule." YouTube. November 6, 2020. Video. https://www.youtube.com/watch?v=PcDeoTKGXcw.

The above links are available at:

sites.broadviewpress.com/ethicsprimer/chapter-6

7
Reflections
on the Ethical Lenses

We have surveyed four distinct approaches to ethics that focus on different things: consequences; actions (and duties); character (and virtues); and relations. Within each of these approaches, there are various lines of thought. Consequentialist approaches might value different ends and have different views about who counts and how to count them. Deontological approaches may ground duties on social roles, past actions, or reason alone. Virtue ethics approaches have disparate ideals of the good life or living well. Relational approaches attend to different types of relationships and how they inform what we should do.

Although the specific theories and concepts we have canvassed are well-known in philosophical ethics, the descriptions given here are simply the bare bones and significantly incomplete. In some cases, particularly the *Bhagavad Gita* (section 4.1 duties based on social role) and Confucianism (section 6.1 focus on personal relations), we have simply taken an idea that exemplifies the type of approach of interest to us while ignoring important doctrines and theories associated with these texts. The Asian traditions, in particular, are vast and have sufficiently many distinct schools within them that authoritative categorization under these lenses is impossible. Nonetheless, in their application to moral life, these differences between schools often boil down to focusing (more or less) on consequences, actions, character (and virtues), or relations.

You may also have noticed that many of these philosophical schools are continuous with religious traditions, each with their own account of the origin of the universe, the character of the beings in the universe, and their moral status. This is obvious in, say, Indigenous and Buddhist philosophy, but is no less true of the Christian basis of Kant's ethics or the Greek pagan foundations of Aristotelianism. Twentieth-century philosophers in the European tradition have tended to downplay the religious aspects of various ethical theories and foregrounded those features that can be understood and justified from a secular perspective. It is an open question how successful these efforts have been. However, for applied ethics in free societies, this kind of approach is essential. After all, as explained in the discussion of public reason (section 2.4), it's unreasonable to expect others to conform to our religious beliefs, so we had better have non-sectarian justifications for our judgements if we are to make ethical decisions that affect more than just ourselves.

Not unrelatedly, many of the theories we have discussed are in some ways ethically fraught and have proponents that are, to say the least, morally imperfect. Kant and early proponents of Kantianism clearly supported Eurocentrism, scientific racism, and had a part in the whitewashing of philosophy in the European tradition.[1] Aristotle famously defended slavery and the inherent inferiority of women.[2] Similarly, traditional Confucians clearly placed women in a subordinate relation to men.[3] The idea of duties based on social roles, discussed in the *Bhagavad Gita*, is sometimes associated with religiously informed social stratification in India[4] and although the Mohists advocated for and supported small Chinese states in their defence against aggressors,[5] we may well wonder if their principles are consistent with individual freedom. And so on.

The lesson here is not to give up on ethics. As should by now be clear, that's not really possible anyway. Rather, the lesson is to treat each theory, text, and theorist with critical respect rather that unreflective deference. Recognizing the ethical failings of some of our greatest moral leaders and theorists should help us find the courage to honestly assess our own moral failings and help us develop critical tools for figuring out how to do better.

Although we have only offered a flavour of what is out there, we hope it is clear that ethics is, and always has been, a truly global pursuit and, moreover, that there are both remarkable commonalities across many cultural traditions along with striking differences. In a multicultural, global society that is struggling to move beyond its colonial past, it is important not to overlook voices that have valuable ethical insights and can add to our ethical discourse. Moreover, given the extraordinary ethical challenges that face the human species, we not only need every possible theoretical tool at our disposal, but we need every person to feel they have a place in the conversation and a stake in the outcome.

At the same time, we now have some practical tools for thinking about ethical questions. As we noted at the beginning of this primer, ethics starts with the question "What should I do?" Now, when considering your various options, you can apply each lens to see how it directs your attention to the consequences, the nature of the action and your motivations, your own character and who you want to be, and your various relationships and how they constrain and inform your options.

Part III

BEYOND THE
ETHICAL LENSES

Some ethical concepts defy easy categorization under one or other of the ethical lenses and in this part, we will consider two such cases—*rights* and **ahimsa**. While the current dominant conception of rights that has been embraced globally in documents like the United Nations' Universal Declaration of Human Rights originates in the ethical, political, and legal traditions of Europe (particularly, Kantian ethics [discussed above in section 4.3] and social contract theories [mentioned below, section 10.1]), rights discourse has become somewhat detached from these theories. We will only touch on a few key components of rights discourse, but it's useful to be conversant in these basic concepts as people often end up talking about rights in ethical disputes. What will become evident are the limitations of rights and their dependence on more robust and nuanced ethical theories.

Rather than being somewhat detached from the four ethical lenses, *ahimsa* touches on all of them. *Ahimsa*—commonly translated as "nonviolence"—originates from the philosophical and religious traditions of South Asia and has been a guiding principle in multiple social justice movements. Avoiding the harmful consequences of violence, criticizing the motives and nature of violent action, cultivating a nonviolent character, and attending to the relationships produced by violence and nonviolence are all central to *ahimsa*. No one of them is more fundamental or prior to any other. By considering both *ahimsa* and rights, we can see both the power and the limitations of the ethical lens approach.

8
Ahimsa

Ahimsa has been an important moral principle in South Asia for thousands of years and plays a significant role in the traditions of Jainism, Hinduism, Buddhism, and, some would say, Sikhism. Although each of these traditions frames the importance of *ahimsa* and its application in rather different ways, all extend *ahimsa* beyond humans alone. The basic idea is that **himsa**, commonly translated as "violence," should be avoided whenever possible. "Violence" here is to be understood as the act of harming, whether intentionally and directly (say, through injuring another being), intentionally and indirectly (say, through directing someone else to injure another being), or unintentionally (say, by acting or failing to act in a way that injures another being).

As Gandhi scholar Veena Howard notes, "Unlike any other religion, ahimsa defines Jainism."[1] In the Jain tradition, all beings are thought to have **jivas** (or souls) that, in their embodied forms, can experience harm. According to the Jain Sutras:

> All living beings desire happiness, and have revulsion from pain
> and suffering. They are fond of life, they love to live, long to live....
> Hence no living being should be hurt, injured, or killed.... All
> things breathing, all things existing, all things living, all things
> whatsoever, should not be slain, or treated with violence, or
> insulted, or tortured, or driven away.... [Anyone] who hurts living

beings ... or gets them hurt by others, or approves of hurt caused
by others, augments the world's hostility towards [themselves].²

For Jains, all beings are categorized based on the number of senses they possess. Humans and other animals possess the most, with five senses, while
plants only possess one. The more senses a being has, the more ways in
which they are vulnerable to harm and the greater the injury that can be
done to them through violence.

Jains recognize four types of *himsa*: defensive violence; violence brought
about through one's profession; violence brought about through one's activities of daily living; and intentional violence. They recognize that complete
ahimsa is impossible but, nonetheless, strive to achieve it. Jain monks and
nuns avoid *all* forms of violence, so they will, for instance, gently sweep the
path ahead of them, so as to avoid stepping on any insects. When confronted
with violence, they refrain from violent self-defence and many will not pre-
pare their own food or have food prepared for them but only accept food as
a gift. For Jain laypeople, however, *ahimsa* isn't as strict and includes conduct
such as adopting vegetarian or vegan diets and avoiding occupations and
situations that may involve violence.

It is important to note that *ahimsa* does not imply passivity. It is not
just the negation of violence but can involve acting in creative ways that are
free of violence and that promote a future free from violence. Some contemporary peace advocates argue that nonviolence can offer a comprehensive
normative framework as a guide to personal and political action.³ Indeed, a
number of leaders in social justice movements have been inspired by *ahimsa*,
notably Mohandas Gandhi, in the struggle for Indian self-rule, and Martin
Luther King Jr., who was a key leader in the US civil rights movement of the
1950s and 1960s.⁴

While *ahimsa* draws attention to each of the four lenses considered
above, it does not focus on any one lens more than another. Clearly, *ahimsa*
is consequentialist as it begins from the notion that causing harm is ethically wrong. Anything that you might do that would result in another being's
injury should be avoided. However, *ahimsa* is also deontological. The motivations behind our actions must align with nonviolence. It is not enough to
have nonviolent deeds; nonviolent words and thoughts are also required. We
should intend peace, compassion, and nonviolence because, in a way, these
actions are good in and of themselves.

Importantly, *ahimsa* does not just refer to ethical codes of conduct, but
also the virtues that allow one to live harmoniously both within one's society
and with oneself. *Ahimsa* and the related habits of mind and emotions, like

compassion, must be cultivated. Gandhi believed that *ahimsa* was intimately tied to the virtue of self-control—absolute nonviolence to all living creatures requires one to conquer the seductions of the ego and exercise restraint.[5] Lastly, *ahimsa* is relational. A commitment to *ahimsa* draws attention to the ways in which beings are interconnected with each other and vulnerable to harm from each other. Because of these interconnections and the negative effects that violence has on one's own character, any violence towards a living being results in violence towards oneself.

Stop and Think

Suppose that all humans made a commitment to live (as best they could) according to *ahimsa*.

What ethical challenges would be solved by living in a way that's committed to *ahimsa*?

What ethical challenges would arise?

Chapter 8 Quiz

1. Which of the following is not one of the forms of *himsa* mentioned in the *Applied Ethics Primer*?
   a. Violence brought about through bad luck
   b. Violence brought about through one's activities of daily living
   c. Defensive violence
   d. Violence brought about through one's profession
   e. Intentional violence

2. True or False: *Ahimsa* only refers to passive nonviolence.

Further Reading

In addition to the sources in the endnotes, the following may be helpful:

"Buddhism and Jainism." In *Buddhism and Jainism*, edited by K.T.S. Sarao and Jeffery D. Long. Dordrecht: Springer, 2017.
    See entry on "Ahimsa," pp. 19–36.
Fiala, Andrew. *Nonviolence: A Quick Immersion*. New York: Tibidabo, 2020.
    See pp. 26–30.

Howard, Veena R. "Nonviolence and Justice as Inseparable Principles: A Gandhian Perspective." In *Justice and Mercy Will Kiss: Paths to Peace in a World of Many Fails*, edited by Michael K. Duffey and Deborah S. Nash, 135–43. Milwaukee: Marquette University Press, 2008.

Miller, Christopher J., and Jonathan Dickstein. "Jain Veganism: Ancient Wisdom, New Opportunities." *Religions* 12, no. 7 (2021): 512–22. https://doi.org/10.3390/rel12070512.

Skaria, Ajay. "Ahimsa." In *Key Concepts in Modern Indian Studies*, edited by Rachel Dwyer, Gita Dharampal-Frick, Monika Kirloskar-Steinbach, Jahnavi Phalkey, 5–7. New York: New York University Press, 2015.

The above links are available at:

sites.broadviewpress.com/ethicsprimer/chapter-8

9
Rights
and Privileges

Unlike some of the moral theories discussed so far, everyone who is reading this primer is likely familiar with the term "rights." For example, you might have heard of human rights, property rights, or even used phrases like "It's my right!" in arguments of your own. In its most general sense, a right is simply a claim made against another, thus, insofar as most moral theories imply various claims we have against each other they involve *rights* in this thin sense. In this section, we focus on the narrower, more substantive sense of rights. It is important to be aware of the two uses of the term, however, as some disputes may rest on equivocations between these two senses.

While the term "right" is often deployed in legal contexts, as with documents like the *Canadian Charter of Rights and Freedoms*, our focus is on moral rights. **Legal rights** are articulated by legal codes and enforced by various legal institutions, whereas **moral rights** are rights that are justified or motivated by moral arguments. In some cases, these rights overlap. After all, one would hope that some legal rights became enforceable by law *because* there are powerful moral reasons to protect them. Through studying ethics, one may come to realize that a particular moral right should be protected by law or that some laws should be scrapped or changed because they are unfair or otherwise unethical. While arguments at the intersection of ethics and law are beyond the scope of this primer, we do note the tendency for discussions of ethical, political, and legal rights to blur into each other.

So, what are rights? **Rights** are entitlements or enforceable claims that we make in relation to others. If one is entitled to a certain right, then other individuals or groups are obligated to protect, fulfill, enforce, or at least not violate that right. Suppose you claim that all people have a right to potable drinking water. Such a right brings with it the responsibility for someone to ensure that any given person has access potable drinking water. In this way, rights generate strong duties that we have to each other. If we fail to respect someone's right to something, then we commit a serious injustice to them. Some philosophers hold that rights override all other moral claims, though this is contentious. As we will see, we often face the challenge of adjudicating among competing rights claims.

9.1 Categorization of Rights

There are several key distinctions that specify different types of rights: negative versus positive rights; active versus passive rights; *in rem* versus *in personam* rights; and the distinction between rights and privileges. Identifying these different types of rights and understanding how they relate to each other helps one assess the character of any given rights claim. Moreover, exploring these distinctions elucidates what rights are and how they relate to the actions of rightsholders and those who ought to respect, protect, and uphold rights.

Negative rights are freedoms that obligate others to not interfere with a rightsholder's actions. For example, you have a right to not be assaulted. This right obligates the rest of us not to physically strike or harm (that is, assault) you. A **positive right**, in contrast, is a right that entitles one to a specific good or service, obligating at least one other person to ensure one's access to that good or service. Consider the right to clean drinking water. This right might obligate a parent to ensure that their child has water to drink or obligate a government to ensure that its citizens have access to safe drinking water. In brief, a positive right requires others to *do* something and a negative right requires that others *not* do (or forebear from doing) something.

Negative rights can be further subdivided into active and passive rights. **Active rights** are the rights one has to act in a way that is free from the interference of others. Conversely, **passive rights** are the rights one holds to not be treated in certain ways. An example of the former is the right to freedom of speech, where one has the right to voice their opinions and say what they believe without someone else silencing them. An example of a passive right is the right to not be discriminated against because of one's cultural, racial, sexual, political, etc. identities.

Notice that active and passive rights can be in tension with each other. One's freedom to act without interference (active) is limited by the freedom of others to not have certain things done to them (passive). So, in the above examples, one's right to freedom of speech is limited by their duty to uphold the right of others to not be discriminated against through actions like hate speech. It is difficult to balance active negative rights with passive negative rights. Different moral theories place different emphases on which rights should override others.

Stop and Think

Can you think of other cases where rights claims might compete?

Another key distinction concerns the identification of who bears the obligations to respect, fulfill, or protect a given right, which is captured by the distinction between *in personam* versus *in rem* rights. **In personam rights** hold against one or more specifiable persons. For example, every person has the right to a safe working environment. Because of the relationship between employer and employee, this means employees hold this right against their employers. Thus, employers have an obligation to their employees to make sure their workplace is safe. On the other hand, **in rem rights** hold against people in general. Recall the right to not be assaulted. This right is not held against specific persons but against anyone and everyone.

9.2   Privileges

Rights—claims that generate correlative duties in other persons or institutions—are contrasted with **privileges** (also called "liberties" or "freedoms"). To have a privilege means that one is free to act (or not act) as they wish, but this freedom is unprotected. This means that it doesn't entail corresponding duties. For example, if you have a driver's license, you have the privilege of being allowed to drive. There is no corresponding duty to ensure that you have the means to drive. No one has a responsibility to provide you with a vehicle and the opportunity to drive it. You are simply free to drive if you have the means. Moreover, you do not have a duty to drive. A privilege is not something you are obligated to do.

Stop and Think

Is education a right or a privilege?

Likely, your answer to this question will depend on the kind or level of education you consider.

If education is a right, what kind of right is it?

9.3   Rightsholders

But, *who* has rights? In most philosophical and political discourses, the existence of a right means that every individual of equal moral status deserves that right. So, for instance, many philosophers would hold that, in virtue of our dignity as human beings, every non-fetal human has a claim to certain rights. (Note, many rights theorists take "dignity" to mean something like the Kantian idea of being an end in itself,[1] discussed above in section 4.3.) However, there are others who hold that various nonhuman entities have rights. Most commonly, some have suggested that those nonhuman animals who have capacities and interests that are much the same as the morally relevant capacities and interests found in humans should share some of the same rights as humans. Here again, we see the issue of moral status. The question of who should have rights and which rights they should have is, in effect, the question of who counts morally, and how we should count them. Grappling with such questions requires ethicists to go back to moral theories (such as those discussed in Part II) to tease out the underlying justification for the rights in question.

9.4   The Function of Rights

Debates about the character and function of rights address questions regarding what rights do for rightsholders.[2] There are two dominant approaches to the function of rights: the will theory and the interest theory. The **will theory** holds that rights pertain to dignified moral agents whose status demands that their agency and **autonomy** be protected by rights. Thus, the main role of rights according to the will theory is to ensure that autonomous individuals have *freedom* over their actions and, importantly, that others have a duty to respect and not violate that freedom. We can see here the Kantian influence on rights discourse as, in effect, rights are thought to protect the autonomy (or "sovereignty") of those individuals deemed ends in themselves. Conversely, the **interest theory** highlights the importance of protecting interests that are critical to one's *well-being*. Here, we might think that consequentialist theories (like utilitarianism) are likely to be the most effective grounds for justifying and elucidating such claims.

While these theories overlap in some of the rights they advocate, the different approaches may interpret these rights in importantly different ways. For instance, both will theorists and interest theorists may think that people have a right to health care. However, the will theorist would likely emphasize the importance of health care for protecting our autonomy and dignity, which may be threatened by illness or injury. In contrast, the interest theorist would view health as one of a set of important interests that are constitutive of one's well-being and flourishing as a person.[3] These different theoretical perspectives will tend to produce very different views of the goals of health care, and on how access to health care should be provided. For example, will and interest theorists may disagree on how much one should be taxed to subsidize the health care system or which areas of the health care system deserve more resources. Both theories are subject to various difficulties and criticisms, and recourse to more basic ethical theory is often required to resolve disputes.

9.5   Objections to a Rights Approach

Despite its ubiquity in moral and especially political discourse, there are a number of difficulties with a rights approach. As noted, rightsholders make claims against others who have corresponding duties. However, it is often difficult to know *who* is obligated to ensure and protect a given right. Consider the claim that all humans have a right to clean drinking water. Whose duty is it to ensure that people in our own community or elsewhere have access to water? Do we have an obligation to our neighbours to ensure that they have potable water? Is the local or national government responsible? Or, does the international community have a responsibility to ensure that all people have access to clean water? If so, does that mean that those of us who are university students and professors have a moral obligation to provide clean water to others across the world? Setting aside the practical problems of motivating people to protect the rights of strangers on the other side of the globe and the political dangers of interfering in another nation's internal politics, the theoretical problem remains of how to determine who should protect this right.

Another difficulty of a rights approach is determining which rights are the most deserving of protection when rights conflict. As mentioned above (section 9.1), it is common for certain active rights to be limited by passive rights. However, this becomes more complicated when interest theorists and will theorists debate the various kinds of rights that ought to be respected, protected, upheld, or prioritized. Both approaches have their weaknesses. Neither has decisive replies to the problems of the other. Typically, intractable debates about competing rights require us to return to the ethical theories that ground them, reserving rights language for political discourses and legal contexts.

Stop and Think

Can you think of a case where an individual or group incorrectly made a rights claim?

Why were they wrong?

Because of the complexity of rights, their limits, and their entailments, many people use rights language incorrectly. Now you have some tools to analyse rights claims in everyday discourse, you should be able to think more critically about what people mean when they say they have a right!

Chapter 9 Quiz

1.   Match the concepts with their description.

Negative rights not to have certain things done to us, sometimes called "security rights."	Privileges
Rights that some hold against people generally.	Active Negative Rights
Unprotected freedoms, meaning that the freedom to act how one wishes doesn't entail corresponding duties in others.	Negative Rights
Rights to someone else's positive action.	Passive Negative Rights
Rights to another person's non-action or forbearance.	*In rem* rights
Negative rights to go about one's own business free from the interference of others.	Positive Rights
Rights that some hold against one (or more) determinate, specifiable person(s).	*In personam* rights

2. True or False: Privileges are protected freedoms, meaning that the freedom to act how one wishes entails corresponding duties in others.

3. True or False: A claim-right is always paired with a corresponding duty or obligation which applies to at least one other person. Violation of my claim-right is always the violation by someone else of their duty towards me.

Further Reading

In addition to the sources in the endnotes, the following may be helpful:

Metz, Thaddeus. "Ubuntu as a Moral Theory and Human Rights in South Africa." *African Human Rights Law Journal* 11, no. 2 (2011): 532–59. https://www.ahrlj.up.ac.za/metz-t.

O'Neill, Onora. "The Dark Side of Human Rights." *International Affairs* 81, no. 2 (March 2005): 427–39. https://www.jstor.org/stable/3568897.

Rainbolt, George W. "Rights." In *Ethics in Practice: An Anthology*, 5th ed., edited by Hugh LaFollette, 53–61. Oxford: Wiley Blackwell, 2020.

Sreenivasan, Gopal. "A Hybrid Theory of Claim-Rights." *Oxford Journal of Legal Studies* 25, no. 2 (July 2005): 257–74. https://doi.org/10.1093/OJLS/GQI013.

Wenar, Leif. "The Nature of Rights." *Philosophy and Public Affairs* 33, no. 3 (July 2005): 223–52. https://doi.org/10.1111/j.1088-4963.2005.00032.x.

Wenar, Leif. "Rights and What We Owe to Each Other." *Journal of Moral Philosophy* 10, no. 4 (January 2013): 375–99. https://doi.org/10.1163/174552412X628968.

The above links are available at:

sites.broadviewpress.com/ethicsprimer/chapter-9

Part IV

FINAL THOUGHTS

Some people think that taking ethics seriously is naïve. Many may worry that if we don't look after our own interests nobody else will. Indeed, we may think that each of us individually is best equipped to make judgements about what will be best for ourselves and resist the idea of offering help or accepting it from anyone else. Some people will defend such views on the basis of claims about the competitive character of human nature, appealing to capitalism or Darwinism (quite mistakenly, we should add), as grounds for thinking that everyone should single-mindedly pursue their own interests and preferences. If we have such an attitude, it is easy to see why we might be predisposed to selfishness. In this final part of the primer, we describe what is often called **rational self-interest** and explain why it may actually require us to think about and protect the interests of others. We then consider some problematic self-regarding attitudes before surveying some helpful heuristics that should help us avoid cognitive biases.

10
Self-Regarding Attitudes

10.1 Selfishness and Self-Interest

All of us are, to some extent, concerned about our own self-interests and, indeed, most of the moral theories canvassed above suggest that we *should* protect our own interests at least as much as everyone else's. However, *selfishness*, understood as simply pursuing one's own preferences and interests without any consideration of the preferences and interests of others, is not only generally considered immoral; it is also irrational.

First of all, it doesn't seem to be psychologically plausible. Almost all of us have some automatic and unavoidable feelings of sympathy and care for some other people. As relational theorists have pointed out, we are social beings who are for large parts of our lives intimately dependent on the good will and care of other people. Indeed, all of us are totally (or at least largely) dependent on others for most of the first couple of decades of our lives and most of us experience such dependency to varying degrees and for varying lengths of time throughout our adulthood. The trust and nurturance that exist in healthy relationships of dependency are important for our emotional well-being. We psychologically benefit from helping each other.

Secondly, if everyone always behaved selfishly the vast majority, and perhaps all of us, would likely be considerably worse off than if we cooperated. This means that selfishly pursuing one's own self-interest would undermine one's self-interest, which is self-defeating. So, rational self-interest requires us to think of others.

Early modern political theorists in the liberal tradition recognized this and generalized from the ethics of personal interactions to the ethical justification of how we structure society and justify the limitations on our personal freedom within society. English philosopher, Thomas Hobbes, identified the situation where everyone simply pursues their own immediate self-interest as a "[war] of every one against every one" where life is "solitary, poor, nasty, brutish, and short."[1] We are better off, thought Hobbes, if we enter into a social contract where we submit to a state power that maintains order. As we have already seen, Mozi had much the same idea. (We might think that *ubuntu* also expresses a similar insight.) Much of political philosophy is committed to trying to figure out the details of this idea.

It is worth noting that even those who tout the virtue of selfishness will typically defend some limits on individual liberty. After all, as we saw in Chapter 9, rights come with corresponding duties. One cannot protect everyone's freedom without limiting people's freedom to act in ways that would limit the freedom of others. Respecting other people's rights inevitably entails curtailing some of our own preferences.

Thinking that everyone should simply pursue their own self-interest and not be asked to look after the interests of others also seems to be substantially unfair. After all, sometimes people are simply unlucky and need help from others through no fault of their own. To find ourselves in a world in which nobody has an obligation to help *us* when we are in terrible need—through sheer misfortune—would not at all serve our preferences and interests. So, our rational self-interest seems to require certain types of altruism and reciprocity.

Of course, you may think that there is no such thing as luck and people have nobody but themselves to blame for their circumstances, so they don't deserve help from anyone else. However, this attitude simply overlooks real facts of life—not merely simple bad luck, but also the reality that there are oppressive political structures that harm people and severely limit their options. The failure to appreciate this reality tends to reflect a certain type of self-oriented thinking that fails to take seriously the challenges in other people's lives or the good luck and privileges of one's own.

10.2 Exceptionalism

Exceptionalism is a form of self-oriented thinking that often undermines ethical decision-making. Exceptionalism is where one believes or acts as if one group (or person) is exempt from following the rules that everyone else must follow or is immune from being judged by the same standards as others. Typically (though not always), exceptionalism is self-serving. We tend to want special treatment for members of our own group, and we may tend to rationalize why the general rules and standards shouldn't apply to us. One of the most common forms of exceptionalism is **nationalism**—though there are many others.

Stop and Think

As mentioned, nationalism is a common type of exceptionalist thinking.

What other kinds of exceptionalism are there?

It is important to remember that exceptionalism is not only a moral failure; it is a rational failure. Exceptionalist thinking treats one group or individual as different from every other when there is, in fact, no relevant difference. Of course, in some cases there may actually be a difference that justifies differential treatment. Sometimes the same rules *shouldn't* apply to everyone equally. Sometimes there *are* relevant facts that entail that it would be *irrational* and *unfair* to treat everyone exactly the same.

After all, we may have a special obligation to the members of a certain group that justifies our placing their interests over others. For instance, a teacher will typically prioritize the learning goals of their own students over those of other students who aren't in their classes. As another example, the members of our group may be systematically treated unfairly in some respects and given this injustice, it may be fairer to give us special opportunities. This is the logic behind most affirmative action initiatives. In such cases, getting clear on the facts is obviously important. Certainly, if one believes that a particular individual or group should be exempt from the rules governing everyone else, then one should expect to be able to give an argument justifying it.

Importantly, exceptionalism may infect the way in which we think about accountability. Particularly within certain groups—like professional organizations, political parties, or religious groups—there is a tendency to think that one is only truly accountable to other members. Immoral actions by corporations are sometimes defended by the claim that their only obligation is to their shareholders, whose only interest is the maximization of profits. This, however, is just a self-serving way of protecting oneself from criticism and is, again, a kind of moral failure. As a general rule, we should think of ourselves as accountable to everyone who is affected by our actions or who has some other interest in our behaviour.

10.3 Moral Licensing

Moral licensing picks out another kind of ethical mistake that is grounded in inappropriate self-regard. This happens when people who have behaved ethically by some measure in the past feel this good behaviour licenses them to behave badly in the present. There is no reason to think this is a conscious or considered decision. Rather, it seems that the good behaviour in the past feeds into a positive self-image that then resists the negative implications of the present behaviour. So, for instance, someone who voted for a Black politician in the past might go on to vote for an overtly racist politician in the present, without thinking that what they are doing is racist.[2] It is as if previous moral behaviour inoculates oneself against current immoral behaviour.

Of course, ethically speaking, such a view is absurd. Moral licensing is best thought of as a cognitive bias. As with other biases, we need to protect ourselves against making this kind of mistake if we hope to behave ethically. As with other emotional or subconscious reactions, the best ways to avoid cognitive biases that lead to unethical behaviour are evaluating decisions using the various ethical lenses discussed above, critical engagement with others who have very different perspectives, and careful reasoning.

Stop and Think

We have identified two kinds of bias—exceptionalism and moral licensing—that may get in the way of moral decision-making.

What are some other types of bias that prevent us from reasoning well about ethical matters?

Chapter 10 Quiz

1. True or False: Exceptionalism is believing or acting as if one group (or person) is exempt from following the rules that everyone else must follow or is immune from being judged by the same standards as others.

2. True or False: Moral licensing is the feeling people have that their past ethical behaviour licenses them to behave badly along the same lines in the present.

Further Reading

In addition to the sources in the endnotes, the following may be helpful:

Gladwell, Malcolm. "The Lady Vanishes." *Revisionist History*. June 16, 2016. Podcast. Accessed November 11, 2022. https://www.pushkin.fm/podcasts/revisionist-history/the-lady-vanishes.

Kavka, Gregory. "The Reconciliation Project." In *Morality, Reason and Truth: New Essays on the Foundations of Ethics*, edited by David Copp and David Zimmerman, 297–319. Totowa, NJ: Rowman & Allanheld, 1984.

Plato. "The Immoralist's Challenge." In *Ethical Theory: An Anthology*, edited by Russ Shafer-Landau, 132–37. Chichester, UK: Wiley-Blackwell, 2012.

Rachels, James. "Ethical Egoism." In *The Elements of Moral Philosophy*, 4th ed., 76–90. New York: McGraw-Hill, 2003.

The above links are available at:

sites.broadviewpress.com/ethicsprimer/chapter-10

11
Helpful Heuristics

Happily, there are a number of **heuristics**—simple, practical strategies—that people have suggested, aimed at resisting the worst tendencies of self-interested biases. For instance, US political philosopher, John Rawls, proposed an interesting way of using rational self-interest to subvert exceptionalist thinking in political theory.[1] He suggested that when we are trying to determine a just solution to a social problem or even what a just society might be, we should imagine ourselves behind a **veil of ignorance**. By this, he meant that when we are trying to decide what social arrangement would be the most just, we should imagine that we don't know what our position or role in society might be. He thought that if we make decisions about social arrangements imagining that we might be in the worst possible position in society, then we will favour fairer decisions.[2] The veil of ignorance heuristic can be extended to thinking about how our own actions might affect or be judged by others but is particularly useful in thinking about policy decisions in various applied ethics contexts.

Many cultures share another kind of tool to guard against self-regarding cognitive biases. In the Christian tradition, it is called the **Golden Rule**: "do to others what you want them to do to you" (Matthew 7:12). Unsurprisingly, the two other major religions which share historical roots with Christianity also have this maxim as central. Jewish law teaches, "Love your neighbour as yourself" (Leviticus 19:18), and we can find much the same idea in Islamic thought.[3] It is perhaps more striking that we can find the same basic idea in India, China, and Africa. In the *Mahabharata*, one passage counsels, "One should not behave towards others in a way which is disagreeable to oneself. This is the essence of morality. All other activities are due to selfish desire."[4] Similarly, Kongfuzi taught, "What you do not want done to yourself, do not do to others."[5] These are just a few examples of the traditions where we can find this important reminder to avoid exceptionalist and selfish thinking.

Of course, the veil of ignorance and the Golden Rule are just heuristics and cannot offer perfect guidance. Some philosophers have complained that our imaginations are limited, and that it is much better to attend to what the least fortunate in our society say they want, rather than imagining ourselves in their shoes. Similarly, you may have some pretty peculiar tastes and preferences, so others may not *want* to be treated the same way as you would like to be. But arguably, such responses risk missing the point. These heuristics are helpful because they remind us that other individuals have lives as rich, complicated, and worthy of respect as our own.

Helpful heuristics aside, some of the best tools for challenging our own cognitive biases and self-interested attitudes have already been described in this primer. It's not just the substance of these ideas and methods that makes them so effective. Employing them slows down our deliberation and decision-making, increasing the likelihood that we will make good, well-considered judgements. Daniel Kahneman, who won the Nobel Prize for his research on human decision-making, describes two ways that most human brains process information and make decisions: **fast thinking** and **slow thinking**.[6] The fast thinking system takes past experiences, judgements, and decisions and unreflectively applies these previous patterns to current situations, thus saving mental effort. Fast thinking is common and effective in daily tasks and decision-making. However, it also makes us susceptible to cognitive biases and errors in thinking, like the self-interested biases discussed above. Slow thinking is the rational and deliberative thought process that allows humans to think critically about their beliefs, values, and experiences when making choices.[7] The slow thinking system requires significant mental effort. But Kahneman has found that—although, as rational agents, we *identify* with the slow thinking process—we depend more on fast thinking. Kahneman's research shows that when we allow our brains to run on autopilot, are cognitively busy or exhausted, or are avoiding tasks that engage our slow thinking processes, then we are more susceptible to selfish, unethical, and even discriminatory behaviour.[8]

Stop and Think

Can you identify a situation in which, on reflection, you behaved badly because you were relying on fast thinking?

How might things have gone differently if you had made time for careful, critical reflection?

Using the tools that we have described in this primer will help you engage your slow thinking processes and avoid the cognitive biases that might lead to unethical attitudes or behaviour. Productive debate and philosophical argumentation can help one understand alternative positions and evaluate the strength of one's own reasons for accepting a given conclusion. The ethical lenses can help one think through decisions about how to act from various perspectives that have different starting points or central commitments. And carefully employing the helpful heuristics described above can disrupt the fast thinking that we subconsciously use to make most of our small, everyday decisions when our choices matter morally. Ethical reflection and discussion helps one think critically about the attitudes, beliefs, and practices we might take for granted—attitudes, beliefs, and practices that may be engrained in our automatic, fast thinking habits.

11.1   Conclusion

These final thoughts ultimately bring us back to the point that we made right at the beginning of this primer in the Introduction. *You cannot avoid ethics.* Whatever path one takes in life, ethical problems will arise, and we will be challenged to determine for ourselves what it means to live well and do the right thing in the circumstances in which we find ourselves. Each of us plays a part in creating more ethical practices in our society and creating a more just community. Different professions and applied ethics contexts come with their own particular challenges, but each can be assessed by employing much the same tools—including the ideas offered in this primer.

Chapter 11 Quiz

1. True or False: The veil of ignorance is the idea that ignorance creates a veil that stops people from behaving ethically.

2. True or False: Our fast thinking system is engaged when we challenge our cognitive biases and make thoughtful, rational decisions.

3. True or False: The best way for making ethical decisions and challenging our self-interested attitudes and harmful biases is by using helpful heuristics.

Additional links for this chapter are available at:

sites.broadviewpress.com/ethicsprimer/chapter11

Appendix A
Tips for
Reading Actively[1]

You'll see when you look at the following tips that following them will mean spending more time on a bit of reading than you might ordinarily. Don't be dismayed! Spending this extra time is necessary for this sort of reading, and will repay you with far better grasp of the material.

1. Pre-reading

Your aim in pre-reading should be simply to get a general sense of the text. You might look up terms that you don't know and flag what you take to be key points or arguments. (It's a good idea to write the definition or explanation of the term in pencil in the margin of the text. This eliminates the need to look it up each time you read.) Don't worry if you don't understand all of the text at this initial stage.

2. Reading

2.1

Your chief aim in reading argumentative writing is to expose the structure that is hidden in the text. You might think of your task as that of providing an outline of the material. Here are two methods you might use for exposing the structure of a passage:

2.1.1 Flagging

- Flagging is a more active correlate of underlining. Flagging should be done in pencil so any flagging which indicates a misunderstanding of the text can be corrected in re-reading. You are encouraged to develop your own system of flags (some people use a combination of question marks, exclamation marks, asterisks, and little faces).
- Here are some flagging suggestions:

Symbol	Meaning
dfn	This is a definition of a term
??	What? I don't get it
=x?	This means what exactly? (it can indicate ambiguity)
why?	Why is this so? (it can indicate hidden assumptions)
		This is important
||	This is very important
{	This is a development and explication
sum	This is a summary of the above
arg A) B)	This is an argument for a position
1) 2)	These are the steps of the argument
concl	Here's a conclusion
e.g.	Here's an example
counter	Here's a counterargument or counterexample

- Brief questions and comments can be jotted down in the margin and you might want to write a few words describing the piece at the beginning of the reading, in effect, a very brief abstract.

- One of the things you'll notice while flagging and re-reading texts that you've flagged is the number of different ways in which arguments are put together. Seeing how different argument structures operate with examples, counterarguments, etc. will help you to decide how to structure your own papers, how to support and defend your own positions.
- Finally, flag thoroughly, but sparingly. If you know what you're supposed to get out of the reading, read for that and related issues. Indiscriminate flagging suggests as little understanding of the text as no flagging at all.

2.1.2 *Note-taking*

- Many people find that they understand more of what they read if they include writing as part of the process of reading. Simply jotting down something—a question, a summary, what you take to be an important quote—is often an aid to active and intelligent reading.
- You might try this: at the top of the page write down the full bibliographical information for the text, then in the margin, keep track of the page numbers in the text and on the page keep brief notes. You might use different colours or divide the page into two sections to differentiate between paraphrasing the text and your reactions to and questions about the text. Use abbreviations, incomplete sentences, drawings, arrows, or whatever. Think of these notes as jogs to your memory rather than as the mere repetition of the text.

2.2

As you read, make sure that you know whether the author is stating their own view, a possible objection, a contrasting view, an objection to a contrasting view, etc. Try to determine the voice of each passage. Read for what is philosophically interesting, don't get distracted by side issues.

2.3

Try not to slide over parts of the text you don't understand.

- If you feel that you've understood the text, sentence by sentence, and yet you realize that you're foggy about the general idea, purpose, method, or conclusion, go back over the text paying more attention to structural cues. Remember, arguments are comprised of premises and conclusions and your task is to discover how the one leads to the other.

- If you understand the general idea, but you don't have a firm grasp on a particular crucial passage, try to solve for the missing pieces. If you know that something is supposed to follow from premises that you do understand, see whether this looks like that conclusion with which you're having difficulty. Or if you are clear on the conclusion, but don't understand the premises, ask yourself what would lead to the conclusion, and see how this is related to the premises that you don't understand.
- The following lists are of words and phrases that tend to indicate parts of arguments.

Conclusions often follow words and phrases like these:

in summary	hence	as a result
thus	accordingly	we may infer
therefore	I conclude that	which shows that
so	consequently	which entails that
it follows that	proves that	which means that
points to the conclusion that	which allows us to infer	which implies that

Premises often follow words and phrases like these:

because	given that	as indicated by
since	granted that	the reason that
for	as shown by	may be inferred from
whereas	inasmuch as	may be derived from
first	otherwise	in lieu of the fact that
in the first place	follows from	
secondly	in the eighteenth place	

3. Re-reading

When you re-read you know enough about the text to read quickly over the parts you think are easy and to slow down for the interesting or difficult parts. You will have specific questions to bring to the text and you will be in an excellent position both to articulate criticisms and to clear up your misunderstandings.

You should know that when you adopt this three-step approach to reading argumentative works, you'll probably find that you are reading much more slowly than you have in the past. But, you'll also be reading much more critically and effectively. Remember that in reading argumentative works you are not simply trying to understand what the author means but you are also trying to put yourself in a position to engage with and assess the text.

Appendix B
Critical Thinking Worksheet
(ARG Assessment)

Breakdown of ARG Assessment

As explained in Chapter 2, it is important to develop the skill of evaluating philosophical arguments. This will not only help us to see where we might agree and disagree with others, but it will also help us make better arguments ourselves. In this appendix, we break down how to apply the ARG conditions using a worksheet for evaluating arguments.[1]

I. Argument
Recall, to evaluate arguments, we must consider both the reasons (premises) that are given and way that they relate to our conclusion. For more information on the ARG conditions, review the discussion in section 2.2.
The basic elements of a good argument are:

A. The premises are **acceptable**.
- We need to ask ourselves if we have good reasons for believing that the reasons given are true or, at least, plausible or likely to be true. If, as in some cases, we don't actually *know* if they are true, then is there any evidence to suggest they might be false?
- Sometimes, premises are so vague or ambiguous that we can't really make a judgement one way or another. Or we may

simply not be in a position to say because we lack the relevant information. In such cases, rather than judging a premise true or false we must consider it undetermined.
- Notice that we need to evaluate the acceptability of each premise individually.

R. The premises are **relevant**.
- We need to ask ourselves whether the premises are actually relevant to determining the truth of the conclusion. For instance, do they provide evidence that supports the truth of the conclusion?
- Again, each premise must be assessed for its relevance to the conclusion, though sometimes the relevance of one premise depends on the others.

G. The premises provide **good grounds** for accepting the conclusion.
- Ultimately, this is the issue that interests us the most. However, while the A and R conditions are essential to deciding it, other considerations may also be helpful.

In this section of the worksheet, list all of the premises (try to list them in a logical order) and then state the conclusion. Next, evaluate the acceptability and relevance of each premise. When doing this, it is often easiest to identify the conclusion first and then look for the reasons offered in support of it.

II. Hidden and Background Assumptions

Many arguments rely on hidden or background assumptions that are required in order to rationally draw the stated conclusion. Sometimes these are just widely known facts or common sense, but at other times they are highly dubious or even clearly false. For example, in the antacid commercial discussed in section 2.2, the advertisers assume that a rose is similar to the human stomach. However, this assumption is highly dubious; if it is to be acceptable it requires empirical justification. Thinking about what an argument tacitly assumes can help us understand what's going wrong with a weak argument and how it might be possible to repair it.

III. Emotive Tone

We must pay attention to the emotive tone of an argument. Language is powerful and emotional appeals can distract from relevant information and persuade people of some claim even when they fail to offer good grounds for accepting it.

Moral arguments are often full of claims about emotional states and we may think that even words like "good" and "bad," "right" and "wrong" have a certain emotive tone. So the point here is to *notice* the emotive tone and to judge whether it is appropriate to the issues under discussion or a distraction that is offered to cover up the fact that there isn't a good argument (i.e., one that has acceptable, relevant premises that provide good grounds for the conclusion) on offer.

IV. Additional Information

What additional information might you need to assess the truth or falsity of the conclusion of the argument? You might need clarity about the meaning of a technical term or you might need some additional factual information. You might decide that in order to come to a decisive judgement about a conclusion you need information that is impossible to discover in principle, in which case, the rational thing to do is to suspend judgement.

V. Good Grounds

Reflect on the work you have done so far and determine whether the premises provide **good grounds** for accepting the conclusion.

- Considering *all* the premises together, is it rational to accept the conclusion? Note that if we reject a premise because it fails the **A** and **R** conditions, then it cannot be part of a set of reasons that provide good grounds for the conclusion.
- Remember, even if the reasons given are both acceptable and relevant, they may fail to provide sufficient grounds for accepting the conclusion. After all, they might not provide the right *kind* of evidence or fail to provide *enough* of it. If this is the case, then the good grounds condition is not satisfied and we should judge the argument a weak one.
- We may find that there are hidden assumptions that are unacceptable or that we need more information in order to accept the conclusion. This would also show that the argument is weak.
- If the premises are acceptable and relevant, and there are no objectionable background assumptions, and all the information we need to assess the conclusion is provided, then we have good grounds and the argument is a strong one.

VI. Counterarguments and Counterexamples

Recall that **dialogic reasoning** is an important part of philosophical reasoning and argumentation. Here you are challenged to see if you can think of possible objections in the form of counterarguments or counterexamples to the argument.

- Interestingly, excellent arguments can have devastating counterarguments or counterexamples.

VII. Summary

Lastly, we need to consider our entire ARG assessment and determine whether the argument (premises and conclusion) is convincing in light of the ARG conditions, background assumptions, emotive tone, and possible objections to the position.

When you evaluate an argument based on the ARG conditions, you have the tools to give an argument yourself for why the argument is or isn't successful.

You may have different responses to an argument that you are evaluating:

1. Do you *strongly agree* with the argument? If so, you must accept the conclusion and be rationally persuaded by it yourself.

2. Do you *agree* with the argument but believe that it could be strengthened with *argument repair*? Which part of the argument is less persuasive, ambiguous, or unsupported? Can you improve the argument, and if so, how?

3. Do you *strongly disagree* with the argument because it doesn't satisfy the ARG conditions? Is there a devastating counterargument or a completely unacceptable hidden assumption? Make sure you have an argument showing why the argument isn't successful.

4. Do you *disagree* with the argument but believe that it could be strengthened with *argument repair*? Which part of the argument is unconvincing, unsupported, or difficult to rationally accept? Can you improve the set of premises so that they are better able to meet the ARG conditions, and if so, how?

5. Perhaps, you find it difficult to make up your mind as to whether the argument is a good one. If you are *uncertain and need more information* about the argument to make a decision, what kind of information would you need? Why?

The worksheet itself is provided on pages 116–17, and can also be down-loaded from the companion website at:

**sites.broadviewpress.com/ethicsprimer/
critical-thinking-worksheet**

Worksheet

I. Argument (List the premises of the argument.)	Are the premises acceptable and relevant?
State the conclusion.	

II. Does the argument contain any HIDDEN or BACKGROUND ASSUMPTIONS?	Are the assumptions acceptable and relevant?

III. What is the EMOTIVE TONE of your argument? (Are there overly strong appeals to emotion? Is emotionally strong language used to unfairly describe the author's opponent or appeal to the reader?)

IV. ADDITIONAL INFORMATION NEEDED? (Are you missing any premises, or should you clarify terms?)

V. Do you have GOOD GROUNDS for accepting the premises and conclusion? Explain.

VI. Can you think of COUNTERARGUMENTS and COUNTEREXAMPLES to the argument? (i.e., Objections)

VII. SUMMARY: Based on your assessment, evaluate the argument and explain your choice. (Do you strongly agree; agree with repair; need more info; disagree with repair; strongly disagree?)

Notes

Part I: Intro

1   For a short video on the "is/ought problem," check out Nigel Warburton, "The Is/Ought Problem," BBC, last modified November 18, 2014, https://www.bbc.co.uk/programmes/p02c7css.

2   Susan Sherwin, "Foundations, Frameworks, Lenses: The Role of Theories in Bioethics," *Bioethics* 13, no. 3/4 (1999): 198–205.

Chapter 1

1   Tacitus, *The Germany and the Agricola of Tacitus* (Project Gutenberg, 2013), Agricola para. 42, https://www.gutenberg.org/files/7524/7524-h/7524-h.htm.

2   Notice that restrictive views about who counts morally may lead us to exclude some nonfetal humans too, such as the very young and some of the very old, so such restrictive approaches to moral status may turn out to have unacceptable implications.

Chapter 2

1   Monty Python, "Argument Clinic—Monty Python—The Secret Policeman's Balls," YouTube, January 21, 2009, video, https://www.youtube.com/watch?v=DkQhK8O9Jik.

2   Trudy Govier, *A Practical Study of Argument*, Enhanced Edition (Boston: Wadsworth, 2014), 87–103.

3   Retrobox, "Pepto Bismol Rose (1992)," YouTube, November 17, 2012, video, https://www.youtube.com/watch?v=VGRtg6W6Kug.

4   Shannon Dea has an interesting chapter that takes an argument repair approach to abortion debates by suggesting harm reduction as a common value shared by pro-life and pro-choice advocates and then seeing what follows ("A Harm Reduction Approach to Abortion," in *Without Apology: Writings on Abortion in Canada*, ed. Shannon Stettner [Edmonton: Athabasca University Press, 2016], 317–32, https://uwspace.uwaterloo.ca/bitstream/handle/10012/11165/Stettner_2016-Without_Apology.pdf?sequence=1&isAllowed=y#page=327).

5   See Catherine Hundleby for more discussion on argument repair: https://chundleby.com/2015/01/16/what-is-argument-repair.

6   This is also fallacious (illogical) reasoning known as attacking a straw figure. If we misrepresent someone's account so that it is easier to refute, we are not working productively or collaboratively to repair the argument. See the School of Thought's "thou shalt not commit logical fallacies" for more logical fallacies to avoid in your reasoning and writing (https://yourlogicalfallacyis.com/).

7   JeeLoo Liu, *An Introduction to Chinese Philosophy: From Ancient Philosophy to Chinese Buddhism* (Oxford: Blackwell, 2006), 108.

8   Chris Fraser, "Mohism," in *The Stanford Encyclopedia of Philosophy* (Fall 2020 Edition), ed. Edward N. Zalta, §3, last modified November 6, 2015, https://plato.stanford.edu/archives/fall2020/entries/mohism/.

Chapter 3

1   Chris Fraser, "Mohism," in *The Stanford Encyclopedia of Philosophy* (Fall 2020 Edition), ed. Edward N. Zalta, last modified November 6, 2015, https://plato.stanford.edu/archives/fall2020/entries/mohism/.

2   Mozi, quoted in JeeLoo Liu, *An Introduction to Chinese Philosophy: From Ancient Philosophy to Chinese Buddhism* (Oxford: Blackwell, 2006), 110–11.

3   Mozi, *Chinese Philosophy*, 114.

4   Mozi, *Chinese Philosophy*, 116.

5   Fraser, "Mohism," §7.

6   Jeremy Bentham, *An Introduction to the Principles of Morals and Legislation*, ed. Jonathan Bennett (Early Modern Texts, 2017), 6, https://www.earlymoderntexts.com/assets/pdfs/bentham1780.pdf.

7   Bentham, *Principles of Morals*, 22–23.

8   John Stuart Mill, *Utilitarianism* (Project Gutenberg, 2004), chapter 2, para. 6, https://www.gutenberg.org/files/11224/11224-h/11224-h.htm.

9   Bentham, *Principles of Morals*, 144.

10 Elisabeth Boetzkes and Wilfrid Waluchow, *Readings in Health Care Ethics* (Peterborough: Broadview, 2002), 12–13.

11   Notice that this is not the same as the **tragedy of the commons** because we are imagining that one person, not everyone, is acting in their own self-interest and attempting to free ride. See https://www.youtube.com/watch?v=lj_gLquca7Q for more information on commons tragedies.

12   Boetzkes and Waluchow, *Health Care Ethics*, 16.

Chapter 4

1   Stephen Mitchell, trans., *Bhagavad Gita: A New Translation* (New York: Three Rivers Press, 2000), 51–52.

2   W.D. Ross, *The Right and the Good* (Indianapolis: Hackett, 1988), 21–22.

3   Ross, *Right and Good*, 18–36.

4   When students are first introduced to Kantian deontology, they commonly misunderstand the Formula of Universal Law as consequentialist. They think that willing a maxim helps us see what problematic consequences might *result from* the maxim if it was universalized. However, Kant emphasizes that this test is grounded in our reason. We are using it to find logical inconsistencies in our motivations. This test helps us uncover morally problematic motivations that would lead us to do the wrong thing.

5   It is important that when you attempt to follow the Formula of Universal Law you try to make the maxim as generalizable as possible. Often, students think that if they create a specific maxim, such as, "Can I lie about how good my grandmother's haircut looks if she asks me this Friday?" then it is easy to pass Kant's test. However, this move loses sight of Kant's bigger picture: to identify universal moral principles that should guide any autonomous being to act because the action is *intrinsically good*.

6   Immanuel Kant, *Fundamental Principles of the Metaphysic of Morals*, trans. Thomas Kingsmill Abbott (Project Gutenberg, 2004), §1, https://www.gutenberg. org/ebooks/5682. (Slightly amended for gender inclusion.)

7   As a point of interest, Kant has four formulations of the Categorical Imperative— all of which help us rationally decide what we should do. Many Kantian scholars argue that the formulas make the moral law stronger, and, with each progression, subsequent formulations unite the previous ones within it. The *Formula of Autonomy* is "the Idea of the will of every rational being as a will that legislates universal law" (*Groundwork*, 4:432). The fourth formulation, also known as the *Kingdom of Ends*, is "act in accordance with the maxims of a member giving universal laws for a merely possible kingdom of ends" (*Groundwork*, 4:439). For more information on the other formulations, see R. Johnson and A. Cureton's entry in *The Stanford Encyclopedia of Philosophy* on "Kant's Moral Philosophy" (https:// plato.stanford.edu/entries/kant-moral/#AutFor).

8   Immanuel Kant, *Groundwork for the Metaphysics of Morals*, trans. Allen Wood (London: Yale University Press, 2002), 4:429.

Chapter 5

1   The BBC has a nice little video about *eudaemonia* and Aristotle's ethics, which you can view online. See Nigel Warburton, "Aristotle on 'Flourishing,'" BBC, March 2015, video, https://www.bbc.co.uk/programmes/p02n2bhz.

2   Aristotle, *Ethics*, trans. J.A.K. Thomson (London: Penguin Classics, 1976), 1115a6–1116a17.

3   Aristotle, *Ethics*, 1124a1.

4   Aristotle, *Ethics*, 1125b31–3.

5   John M. Koller, *Asian Philosophies*, 5th ed. (Upper Saddle River, NJ: Prentice-Hall, 2002), 53.

6   Koller, *Asian Philosophies*, 59–61.

Chapter 6

1   John M. Koller, *Asian Philosophies*, 5th ed. (Upper Saddle River, NJ: Prentice-Hall, 2002), 220.

2   Koller, *Asian Philosophies*, 222. Confucianism is a good example of an ethical theory that employs many of the different approaches we have discussed here. From these filial relationships come specific duties. The humaneness that follows from filial piety is, in effect, a virtuous character, which is valuable (in part) because it brings about good consequences.

3   Harold D. Lasswell, *Politics: Who Gets What When How* (New York: Whittlesey House, McGraw-Hill Book Co., 1936).

4   Kimberlé Crenshaw, "Mapping the Margins: Intersectionality, Identity Politics, and Violence against Women of Color," *Stanford Law Review* 43, no. 6 (1991): 1241–99.

5   Anne-Marie Callus and Amy Camilleri-Zahra, "'Nothing about Us without Us': Disabled People Determining Their Human Rights through the UNCRPD," *Mediterranean Review of Human Rights* 1 (2017): 1–26, https://www.um.edu.mt/library/oar/bitstream/123456789/56964/1/MHRR1A1.pdf.

6   Michael Onyebuchi Eze, "I Am Because You Are," *UNESCO Courier* (2011): 11–13, https://en.unesco.org/courier/octobre-decembre-2011/i-am-because-you-are.

7   Desmond Tutu, et al., *Truth and Reconciliation Commission of South Africa Report*, vol. 1 (South Africa: Government of National Unity, 1998), 125–28, https://www.justice.gov.za/trc/report/.

8   Yvonne Mokgoro, "Ubuntu and the Law in South Africa," *Potchefstroom Electronic Law Journal* 1, no. 1 (1998): 18, https://www.ajol.info/index.php/pelj/article/view/43567.

9   Tutu, *Truth and Reconciliation*, 128.

10 Mokgoro, "Ubuntu," 24–25.

11 Mokgoro, "Ubuntu," 19.

12   Margaret Robinson, "Animal Personhood in Mi'kmaq Perspective," *Societies* 4 (2014): 672–88, https://www.mdpi.com/2075-4698/4/4/672.

13   John Borrows, *Seven Generations, Seven Teachings Ending the Indian Act* (West Vancouver: National Centre for First Nations Governance, 2008), https://fngovernance.org/wp-content/uploads/2020/05/john_borrows.pdf; Linda Clarkson, Vern Morrisette, and Gabriel Régallet, *Our Responsibility to the Seventh Generation: Indigenous Peoples and Sustainable Development* (Winnipeg: International Institute for Sustainable Development, 2001), https://www.iisd.org/publications/our-responsibility-seventh-generation; "Seven Generations—the Role of Chief," PBS, https://www.pbs.org/warrior/content/timeline/opendoor/roleOfChief.html.

14   Clarkson, Morrisette, and Régallet, *Seventh Generation*, 12.

15   Academic Algonquin, "Seven Generations," YouTube, May 18, 2017, video, https://www.youtube.com/watch?v=wHg3enCCyCM.

Chapter 7

1   Peter K.J. Park, *Africa, Asia, and the History of Philosophy: Racism in the Formation of the Philosophical Canon, 1780–1830* (Albany, NY: State University of New York Press, 2013).

2   María Luisa Femenías, "Women and the Natural Hierarchy in Aristotle," *Hypatia* 9, no. 1 (1994): 164–72.

3   Xinyan Jiang, "Confucianism, Women, and Social Contexts," *Journal of Chinese Philosophy* 36, no. 2 (2009): 228–42.

4   Richard H. Davis, "Gandhi, Krishna and Caste, Inequality More or Less," in *Equality More or Less*, ed. Robert E. Tully and Bruce Chiltern, 221–43 (Lanham, MD: Rowman and Littlefield, 2020).

5   Li Bin, "Insights into the Mozi and Their Implications for the Study of Contemporary International Relations," *Chinese Journal of International Politics* 2, no. 3 (2009): 421–54.

Chapter 8

1   Veena R. Howard, "Nonviolence in the 3 Dharma Traditions: Hinduism, Jainism, and Buddhism," in *Routledge Handbook of Pacifism*, ed. Andrew Fiala (New York: Routledge, 2018), 81.

2   Howard, "Nonviolence," 81.

3   Andrew Fiala, "Pacifism," in *The Stanford Encyclopedia of Philosophy*, ed. Edward N. Zalta (Fall 2021 Edition), last modified September 15, 2018, https://plato.stanford.edu/archives/fall2021/entries/pacifism.

4   "Nonviolence," in *Martin Luther King, Jr. Encyclopedia*, https://kinginstitute.stanford.edu/encyclopedia/nonviolence.

5   Howard, "Nonviolence," 89–90.

Chapter 9

1   Leif Wenar, "Rights," in *The Stanford Encyclopedia of Philosophy*, ed. Edward N. Zalta (Spring 2021 Edition), last modified February 24, 2020,§6.1, https://plato.stanford.edu/archives/spr2021/entries/rights.

2   Wenar, "Rights," §2.2.

3   John D. Arras, "The Right to Health Care," in *Routledge Philosophy Companions: Routledge Companion to Bioethics*, ed. John D. Arras, Rebecca Kukla, and Elizabeth Fenton (Florence, KY: Taylor and Francis, 2014), 7.

Chapter 10

1   Thomas Hobbes, *Leviathan* (Project Gutenberg, 2013), chapter 8, https://www.gutenberg.org/files/3207/3207-h/3207-h.htm.

2   The 92nd Street Y, New York, "Malcolm Gladwell on Racism, Trump, and the Moral Licensing Phenomenon," YouTube, June 15, 2016, video, https://www.youtube.com/watch?v=rjf8b_LLZ6g. See also Anna Merritt, Daniel Effron, and Benoît Monin, "Moral Self-Licensing: When Being Good Frees Us to Be Bad," *Social and Personality Psychology Compass* 4/5 (2010): 345–46.

Chapter 11

1   John Rawls, *Justice as Fairness: A Restatement*, ed. Erin Kelly (Cambridge: Harvard University Press, 2001).

2   The BBC has a nice brief introduction to this thought experiment. See Nigel Warburton, "The Veil of Ignorance," BBC, April 2015, video, https://www.bbc.co.uk/programmes/p02n3sgv.

3   For example, see Justin Parrot, "Al-Ghazali and the Golden Rule: Ethics of Reciprocity in the Works of a Muslim Sage," *Journal of Religious and Theological Information* 16, no. 2 (2017): 68–72, http://dx.doi.org/10.1080/10477845.2017.128 1067.

4   Richard H. Davis, "A Hindu Golden Rule, in Context," in *The Golden Rule: The Ethics of Reciprocity in World Religions*, ed. Jacob and Bruce Chilton (London: Continuum, 2008), 146–56.

5   Confucius, *The Analects* (New York: Open Road Integrated Media, 2016), xv, 23, https://ebookcentral.proquest.com/lib/dal/detail.action?docID=4697581.

6   Daniel Kahneman, *Thinking Fast and Slow* (Toronto: Anchor Canada, 2013), 10–12.

7   Kahneman, *Thinking*, 21.

8   Kahneman, *Thinking*, 37.

Appendix A

1   This appendix is a modified version of Karen Pilkington's worksheet "Suggestions as to How to Read Philosophy."

Appendix B

1   This tool was adapted from Priscilla Agnew's "Critical Thinking Worksheet"(Conference paper presentation, 4th Annual International Conference on Critical Thinking and Educational Reform, Sonoma, CA, August 3–6, 1986) and Trudy Govier's *Practical Study of Argument*, Enhanced Edition (Boston: Wadsworth, 2014). For practice questions and a deeper explanation of how to use and apply the ARG conditions, see Chapter 4 of Govier's *Practical Study of Argument*, "Good Arguments: An Introduction."

Solutions to Chapter Quizzes

Chapter 1

1. A
2. True
3. False; remember, a normative question asks what we ought to (or should) do; it is contrasted with descriptive questions.

Chapter 2

1. True
2. False
3. True
4. False

Chapter 3

1. True.
2. False; this isn't quite right because one could achieve "the greatest good for the greatest number" by inflicting abject misery on a few. The utilitarian calculus needs to take into consideration negative utility as well as positive utility.

   3. False

   4. True

Chapter 4

1. False; not all duties that one has due to one's social role are duties of trust.

2. prima facie

3. d; statement c implies consequentialist thinking, suggesting that the ends justify the means, which is contrary to Kantian ethics.

4. c

5. False

Chapter 5

1. b

2. True

3. False

4. b, d, e, and f

Chapter 6

1. False

2. True

3. True

4. False

5. False

Chapter 8

1. a

2. False

Chapter 9

1.

Negative rights not to have certain things done to us, sometimes called "security rights."	→	Passive Rights
Rights that some hold against people generally.	→	*In rem* rights
Unprotected freedoms, meaning that the freedom to act how one wishes doesn't entail corresponding duties in others.	→	Privileges
Rights to someone else's positive action.	→	Positive Rights
Rights to another person's non-action or forbearance.	→	Negative Rights
Negative rights to go about one's own business free from the interference of others.	→	Active Rights
Rights that some hold against one (or more) determinate, specifiable person(s).	→	*In personam* rights

2. False
3. True

Chapter 10

1. True
2. True

Chapter 11

1. False
2. False
3. False; helpful heuristics are good shortcuts, but the best tools we have for making ethical decisions is philosophical argumentation, engaging in productive debates with others, and using the various ethical lenses to evaluate our options and decisions.

Glossary

Numbers in parentheses indicate the part, chapter, or section number in which each term is introduced. Some terms are associated with complete parts or complete chapters of the book.

Active rights
The rights one has to act in ways that are free from the interference of others (9.1)

Ahimsa
Non-harm or nonviolence; a principle that is important in many South Asian traditions (III)

All my/our relations
A teaching shared by a number of peoples indigenous to what settlers call North America that emphasizes how one must consider and respect their relation to other living and non-living beings (6.4)

Applied ethics
A branch of moral philosophy that draws from normative moral theories and concepts to elucidate and resolve ethical problems in real-world situations (I)

Argument repair
The process by which interlocutors amend and improve an argument in light of feedback and constructive critique (2.3)

Autonomy
Capacity for self-governance; the ability to act in accordance with one's preferences, beliefs, and desires (4.3, 9.4)

Beneficence
Doing good or producing benefit (4.2)

Care ethics
A feminist ethic that emphasizes our vulnerability and dependence on one another and argues that these relationships should be central to ethical considerations (6.1)

Categorical Imperative
A fundamental moral principle, developed by Immanuel Kant, that emphasizes the centrality of reason and freedom in defining the moral law and right action (4.3)

Conclusion (of an argument)
A claim that someone attempts to defend by offering various reasons (premises) (2.1)

Confucianism
A philosophical school based on the work of Kongfuzi (Confucius) that (among other things) emphasizes the importance of developing ethical capacities from our relationships with our parents and families (6.1)

Cultural relativism
The view that holds what is ethical or unethical is relative to each culture's norms, beliefs, and practices (2.4)

Deontology
Duty ethics; or an approach to ethics concerned with the intrinsic morality of a choice, action, or intention (4)

Descriptive

A modifier that picks out claims that describe how the world is; often contrasted with "normative" (I)

Dialogic reasoning

When one puts forward one's own view, then comes up with objections to that view, and then responds to those objections (1.2, 2.1)

Dukkha

Dissatisfaction, dis-ease, or suffering, identified by Buddhists as an inescapable part of life (5.2)

Duties of fidelity

Duties to be trustworthy and keep our promises (4.2)

Duties of gratitude

Duties to reciprocate positive actions from others that helped us (4.2)

Duties of reparation

Duties to make amends when we have harmed someone or caused a bad situation (4.2)

Eudaemonia

Aristotle's idea of what makes a good life; translated as "happiness," "well-being," or "flourishing" (5.1)

Exceptionalism

The belief that that one group or person is exempt from following the same rules or standards as everyone else (10.2)

False equivalency

A kind of fallacious (illogical) assertion or argument where one compares two unlike things to make a point, but the things in question are not sufficiently similar to rationally ground the point (2.2)

Fast thinking

The cognitive system that we use for most of our daily decision-making that uses mental shortcuts to make quick decisions (but is more prone to errors because of this) (11)

Fiduciary obligations
Duties that come from particular relations of trust constraining how a professional can act on behalf of their client (4.1)

Filial piety
Attitude of respect for one's parents, elders, and ancestors (3.1)

Formal justice
The idea that like should be treated alike; the impartial, consistent, and strict application of rules (2.4)

Formula of Humanity
A formulation of Kant's Categorical Imperative that states: "So act that you use humanity, as much in your own person as in the person of every other, always at the same time as an end and never merely as a means" (*Groundwork*, 4:429); sometimes referred to as the "Second Formulation" (4.3)

Formula of Universal Law
A formulation of Kant's Categorical Imperative that says, "Act only in accordance with that maxim through which you at the same time can will that it become a universal law" (*Groundwork*, 4:421); sometimes referred to as the "First Formulation" (4.3)

Golden Rule
The principle of treating others as you want to be treated (11)

Heuristics
Mental shortcuts that tend toward error when used uncritically (11)

Himsa
Violence; the act of harming (8)

In personam rights
Rights that hold against one or more specifiable people or groups (9.1)

In rem rights
Rights that hold against *all* people and groups in general (9.1)

Interest theory of rights
The view that rights claims are justified when they would protect interests that are essential for the flourishing of the individual in question (9.4)

Intersectionality
The unique way that individuals experience oppression (and privilege) due to their membership in various social groups (6.2)

Jiva
In the Jain tradition, a *jiva* is a life force or soul (8)

Justice
Fairness or fair treatment (3.2.1, 4.2)

Legal rights
Rights that are articulated and upheld by legal codes and practices (9)

Maxim
A general rule or principle that grounds (and by doing so articulates) the reason for a particular action; see Kant's Formula of Universal Law (4.3)

Mohism
The philosophical school based on the work of Mozi, that emphasizes impartiality and the improvement of society (3.1)

Moral licensing
A tendency to treat ethical behaviour in a given context in the past as giving one license to act unethically at a later time in a similar context (10.3)

Moral rights
Rights that are justified by moral arguments (9)

Moral status
The degree to which different organisms or beings deserve moral consideration; also called *moral standing* or *moral considerability* (II)

Nationalism
The belief that one's nation (and the interests of the nation and its people) should be prioritized over other nations (10.2)

Negative rights
Rights that one holds against the interference of others (9.1)

Non-maleficence
Doing no harm (4.2)

Normative
A modifier that picks out claims that go beyond describing something, they express an evaluation (i.e., something is good or bad). Often contrasted with "descriptive" (I)

Normative ethical theory
The systematic study, development, and rational defence of basic values, moral concepts, and ethical theories (I)

Nothing about us without us
A disability rights slogan that demands the inclusion of individuals with disabilities in designing studies and decision-making that affect people with disabilities; also used by other social justice movements (6.2)

Passive rights
The rights one holds to not be treated in certain ways (9.1)

Paternalism
Restricting someone's autonomy by ignoring or overriding their preferences or decisions; paternalism is often defended by saying that the paternalistic decision is in the best interests of those whose autonomy is overridden (6.2)

Positive rights
Rights that entitle one to a good or service (9.1)

Premise
A statement in an argument that (typically along with other premises) is offered in an attempt to convince others of a specific conclusion (2.1)

Prima facie
Latin for "at first glance" (4.2)

Prima facie duties
Duties that are required unless there is another competing duty that outweighs and overrides it (4.2)

Principle of utility
The principle by which classical utilitarians articulate the good consequences that should be pursued and the bad consequences that should be avoided (3.2)

Privileges
Unprotected freedoms that do not entail corresponding duties in others; also referred to as "liberties" (9.2)

Problem of free riders
Occurs when people use more than their fair share of a benefit or resource without paying their fair share to use it (3.2.1)

Public reason
The idea that ethical rules must be acceptable or justifiable to everyone in a society who is expected to live by these rules (2.4)

Rational self-interest
What is in one's own self-interest all things considered; a rational grounds for self-interested action (IV)

Respect for persons
Protecting and not violating those characteristics of persons (for instance, autonomy) that ground their moral status as persons (4.3)

Rights
Entitlements or enforceable claims we make in relation to others; one individual's rights confer duties on others (9)

Seven generations
A teaching shared by a number of peoples indigenous to what settlers call North America that requires one to consider the previous seven generations and future seven generations in one's decisions and actions (6.4)

Slow thinking
The cognitive system, requiring considerable mental effort, that allows humans to think critically and rationally about their beliefs, values, experiences, and choices when making a decision (11)

The personal is political
A feminist slogan that captures the ways in which our personal situation and actions reproduce (or resist) the structural inequality of our society (6.2)

Theory of knowledge
The branch of philosophy dedicated to understanding the nature, grounds, justification, and limits of knowledge and related concepts; also called "epistemology" (1.2)

Tragedy of the commons
A situation in which a public good is destroyed through many individuals exploiting it, where each individual could rationally justify their action because, on its own, it would not endanger the public good (3.2.1)

Ubuntu
A type of communal ethics that maintains that a person is a person through other people; associated with African ethics and especially South Africa's Truth and Reconciliation process (6.3)

Utilitarianism
The theory of ethics that claims that the utility of consequences is the sole ground for the morality of actions (3.2)

Veil of ignorance
A thought experiment proposed by John Rawls that asks us to imagine that we don't know what our social position would be in society, when we are evaluating the justice of social arrangements within that society (11)

Will theory of rights
The view that rights function to protect the autonomy of persons; rights define individuals as moral agents whose status demands that their agency and autonomy be protected (9.4)

From the Publisher

A name never says it all, but the word "Broadview" expresses a good deal of the philosophy behind our company. We are open to a broad range of academic approaches and political viewpoints. We pay attention to the broad impact book publishing and book printing has in the wider world; for some years now we have used 100% recycled paper for most titles. Our publishing program is internationally oriented and broad-ranging. Our individual titles often appeal to a broad readership too; many are of interest as much to general readers as to academics and students.

Founded in 1985, Broadview remains a fully independent company owned by its shareholders—not an imprint or subsidiary of a larger multinational.

To order our books or obtain up-to-date information, please visit broadviewpress.com.

BROADVIEW PRESS

WWW.BROADVIEWPRESS.COM